Polka Dot Girls

Designed. Original. Treasured.

By
Kristie Kerr & Paula Yarnes

Copyright 2018 Kristie Kerr and Paula Yarnes. All Rights Reserved.

No part of this book may be reproduced, transmitted, or utilized in any form or by any means, graphic, electronic or mechanical, including photocopying, recording, taping, or by any information storage or retrieval, without the permission in writing from the publisher. WITH THE EXCEPTION OF THE POLKA DOT PLUS WEEKLY CHALLENGES, TAKE HOME ACTIVITY SHEETS AND PARENT PARTNERS, WHICH MAY BE DUPLICATED FOR GROUP USE ONLY.

Unless otherwise indicated, all Scripture quotations are taken from the Holy Bible, New Living Translation, copyright © 1996, 2004, 2007 by Tyndale House Foundation. Used by permission of Tyndale House Publishers, Inc., Carol Stream, Illinois 60188. All rights reserved.

THE HOLY BIBLE, NEW INTERNATIONAL VERSION®, NIV® Copyright © 1973, 1978, 1984, 2011 by Biblica, Inc.™ Used by permission. All rights reserved worldwide.

Scripture taken from The Message. Copyright © 1993, 1994, 1995, 1996, 2000, 2001, 2002. Used by permission of NavPress Publishing Group.

Scripture taken from the Contemporary English Version © 1991, 1992, 1995 by American Bible Society, Used by Permission.

Scripture taken from the Common English Bible P.O. Box 801 201 Eighth Avenue South Nashville, TN 37202-0801

Scripture taken from the Holy Bible, NEW INTERNATIONAL READER'S VERSION®. Copyright © 1996, 1998 Biblica. All rights reserved throughout the world. Used by permission of Biblica.

Worldwide English (New Testament) (WE) © 1969, 1971, 1996, 1998 by SOON Educational Publications

ISBN: 978-0-9970676-4-4

Printed in the United States of America

1st Printing

Contents

How to Use this Book vii

What is Self-Control? 1-22
Large Group Lesson 1
Polka Dot Talk
    Kindergarten – 1st Grade 9
    2nd – 3rd Grade 11
    4th – 5th Grade 13
Polka Dot Project 15
Polka Dot Plus
    Parent Partner 16
    Take-Home Activity Sheets
        Kindergarten – 1st Grade 17
        2nd – 3rd Grade 19
        4th – 5th Grade 21

Good Fruit / Bad Fruit 23-46
Large Group Lesson 23
Polka Dot Talk
    Kindergarten – 1st Grade 31
    2nd – 3rd Grade 33
    4th – 5th Grade 35
Polka Dot Project 37
Polka Dot Plus
    Parent Partner 39
    Take-Home Activity Sheets
        Kindergarten – 1st Grade 41
        2nd – 3rd Grade 43
        4th – 5th Grade 45

Mind Control 47-76
Large Group Lesson 47
Polka Dot Talk
    Kindergarten – 1st Grade 53
    2nd – 3rd Grade 55
    4th – 5th Grade 57
Polka Dot Project 59
Polka Dot Plus
    Parent Partner 64
    Take-Home Activity Sheets
        Kindergarten – 1st Grade 65
        2nd – 3rd Grade 69
        4th – 5th Grade 73

Watch Your Mouth 77-102
Large Group Lesson 77
Polka Dot Talk
    Kindergarten – 1st Grade 85
    2nd – 3rd Grade 87
    4th – 5th Grade 89
Polka Dot Project 91
Polka Dot Plus
    Parent Partner 93
    Take-Home Activity Sheets
        Kindergarten – 1st Grade 95
        2nd – 3rd Grade 97
        4th – 5th Grade 101

Money Matters 103-126
Large Group Lesson 103
Polka Dot Talk
    Kindergarten – 1st Grade 111
    2nd – 3rd Grade 113
    4th – 5th Grade 115
Polka Dot Project 117
Polka Dot Plus
    Parent Partner 119
    Take-Home Activity Sheets
        Kindergarten – 1st Grade 121
        2nd – 3rd Grade 123
        4th – 5th Grade 125

Using My Gifts 127-154
- Large Group Lesson 127
- Polka Dot Talk
  - Kindergarten – 1st Grade 135
  - 2nd – 3rd Grade 137
  - 4th – 5th Grade 139
- Polka Dot Project 141
- Polka Dot Plus
  - Parent Partner 143
  - Take-Home Activity Sheets
    - Kindergarten – 1st Grade 145
    - 2nd – 3rd Grade 147
    - 4th – 5th Grade 151

Taking My Time 155-180
- Large Group Lesson 155
- Polka Dot Talk
  - Kindergarten – 1st Grade 163
  - 2nd – 3rd Grade 165
  - 4th – 5th Grade 167
- Polka Dot Project 169
- Polka Dot Plus
  - Parent Partner 170
  - Take-Home Activity Sheets
    - Kindergarten – 1st Grade 171
    - 2nd – 3rd Grade 173
    - 4th – 5th Grade 177

The Way to Obey 181-210
- Large Group Lesson 181
- Polka Dot Talk
  - Kindergarten – 1st Grade 187
  - 2nd – 3rd Grade 189
  - 4th – 5th Grade 191
- Polka Dot Project 193
- Polka Dot Plus
  - Parent Partner 199
  - Take-Home Activity Sheets
    - Kindergarten – 1st Grade 201
    - 2nd – 3rd Grade 205
    - 4th – 5th Grade 209

Your Body, God's House 211-230
- Large Group Lesson 211
- Polka Dot Talk
  - Kindergarten – 1st Grade 217
  - 2nd – 3rd Grade 219
  - 4th – 5th Grade 221
- Polka Dot Project 223
- Polka Dot Plus
  - Parent Partner 224
  - Take-Home Activity Sheets
    - Kindergarten – 1st Grade 225
    - 2nd – 3rd Grade 227
    - 4th – 5th Grade 229

Hands and Feet 231-251
- Large Group Lesson 231
- Polka Dot Talk
  - Kindergarten – 1st Grade 237
  - 2nd – 3rd Grade 239
  - 4th – 5th Grade 241
- Polka Dot Project 243
- Polka Dot Plus
  - Parent Partner 244
  - Take-Home Activity Sheets
    - Kindergarten – 1st Grade 245
    - 2nd – 3rd Grade 247
    - 4th – 5th Grade 249

Dedicated to the girls who inspire us:

Anja who does funny accents…

JoJo who **defies all odds**…

Catelyn who is a SURVIVOR…

Lucy who LOVES unconditionally…

Betty who LIGHTS UP THE ROOM…

Dottie who loves tutus AND **fishing poles**…

Meg who is so funny she could possibly be the next Lucille Ball…

Ling who is NOT AFRAID to speak her mind…

Natalie who can organize like nobody's business…

Jeorgia who has AMAZING COURAGE…

and **Lily** who is simply sweet!

You amaze us.
Go change the world.

How to Use this Book

It seems easy enough, right? Like you really shouldn't need a page just to tell you how to use this book. And yet, here we are. We are nothing if we're not efficient!

Ok. This resource was written as a tool for use in a large group, small group or even for your family to use. Obviously, your specific needs may vary according to the size and make up of your group, but we have hopefully provided you with enough options that you have plenty of…well, options.

Each chapter starts with a large group lesson. This is something that can be taught by one teacher or even a variety of leaders. These lessons are designed to appeal to all age groups – so bring all your girls together for this part of the session. There are stories and illustrations provided, but feel free to add in your own thoughts, insights and stories! The girls will love to hear about your own personal experiences and perspective.

Following the large group time, there are questions for small group discussion. These are broken down by grade level (K-1, 2-3, and 4-5)—so this would be a great time to divide the girls into smaller groups with separate leaders so that the discussion can be tailored to fit their level of experience and understanding. (If you don't have enough leaders to do small groups, keep the girls together and alternate questions from the various age level discussion questions.) Close out your small group time with a time of prayer. Invite the girls to pray for each other and take turns praying out loud. Not only will you learn a lot about your girls during this time, their little hearts will be bonded together when they spend time praying for one another.

Then it's craft time! We've included lots of fun ideas for you to do as a group. Make sure you do adequate preparation depending on the age and skill level of your girls. Nothing is more frustrating than running out of time because you spent too much time cutting things out or waiting for glue to dry. (By the way…glue dries REALLY slow. Even slower when you want it to dry fast. Just our experience anyway…)

Lastly, we've included some pages to be photocopied and sent home. They include age appropriate activity sheets, and a parent partner. These are intended to give the girls some fun tools to work on throughout the week and to let the parents keep up with what their daughters are learning.

And the MOST important thing to remember is to MAKE IT WORK FOR YOU. Every group is unique and different, so feel free to add, subtract, edit, rewrite, and rework anything you find here. Find out what works and stick with it and don't be afraid to chuck the stuff that isn't working.

Our job is simple—but it couldn't be more important. We get the amazing privilege of teaching these sweet girls about Jesus. We pray the material gives you practical tools to do just that. But above and beyond all that, remember that your gift of time and interest in these girls' lives will impact them far greater than any lesson or illustration. You are literally demonstrating for them what it means to be a woman who loves Jesus. Be patient. Be loving. Be fun. Be there.

We wish you all the best as you teach your girls what it means to be a Polka Dot Girl!

Self-Control

week 1

What is Self-Control?

WHAT'S THE POINT?

GOD WANTS TO HELP ME CONTROL MYSELF.

theme verse

So think clearly and exercise self-control.

1 Peter 1:13)

related bible story

Romans 7:15–25

❊ Large Group Lesson ❊

When I was a young girl, I would make the same New Year's resolution every single year without fail. I would sit in my room on December 31 and decide—with everything in my being—that this would be the year that I would reach my goal. I would be victorious! I would be a conqueror! I would do it!

What was this amazing goal, you ask?

Well, every year, I would resolve that ***I would not do anything wrong for an ENTIRE YEAR.***

Yup, you heard me right. No talking back to my parents. No sneaking a cookie after my mom told me I couldn't have one. No fighting with my sister. No talking in class when I wasn't supposed to. No getting into trouble.

You can imagine how far I got into the year before I blew it. Usually until about 9:38 a.m. on January 1. If I lasted even that long.

I would get so disappointed in myself. Why couldn't I do it? Why couldn't I stay out of trouble for at least one measly little day? In my heart, I so desperately wanted to do the right thing all the time, but I found that something inside of me always seemed to take over and I found myself making a bad choice once again.

Have you ever had that happen to you? You know that you shouldn't disobey your parents…you actually really want to honor your mom and dad, yet you find yourself doing the very thing they told you not to do.

Maybe you promise yourself that you're going to stop talking about your friends when they're not around, but then all your other friends start gossiping and you find yourself going along with what everyone else is doing. You leave the conversation wondering, *how did that happen!? I was so sure I was going to do better this time!*

Or maybe you're really trying to not put off your homework so much. You come home from school determined to get your work done right away. But then you turn on the TV or start playing on the computer. Before you know it, your mom is upset with you once again because you forgot to get your homework done. Again.

Why does this happen? How can we be so determined to do the right thing, and then find ourselves failing over and over again?

I asked God this question a few years ago. I was really frustrated with myself because it seemed like no matter how hard I tried, I kept stumbling into the same mistakes over and over again. I really wanted to do the right thing, but something inside of me seemed to fight against it.

And God began to show me that I was making these same mistakes because I wasn't practicing self-

week 1

control. Self-control means…well…controlling yourself! It means MAKING yourself do the right thing at the right time.

I think a lot of you are like me. A lot of my areas of weakness and frustration are directly linked to the fact that I don't control myself. I know the right thing, but I don't do it. I pause and say, "Oh, I shouldn't," but then I go ahead and do it anyway. Or even worse, I don't even realize I'm not practicing self-control! I just don't pay attention. I'm acting without thinking. I'm not stopping to make sure I make good choices.

That—I am beginning to realize—is a dangerous road to be on. These might seem like small little things, but let's be honest: if we cannot control ourselves in the small things, why do we think we can control ourselves in the big things?

I recently read an article about a woman who made a really bad choice that caused a lot of people a whole lot of pain. She said, "I never once thought what I was doing was okay, but I just didn't want to stop."

Wow. Knowing what we should do and not doing it. Facing the choices of right and wrong and not having the self-control to choose the right thing even when your heart and body and mind are telling you to do the wrong thing. This "self-control" stuff is a big, big deal.

I had a friend who used to say, "Sin is saying, 'I'm going to have what I want, when I want it.'" You may have never thought about disobeying your parents as sin, but that's exactly what it is. Sin. Saying, "I know that I shouldn't do this, but I'm going to do it anyway"—no matter how big or how small the issue may be—is a sure sign of a sinful heart.

The Bible tells us we're all born with a sinful nature. There's something inside of us that doesn't want to do the right thing! King David wrote in Psalm 51:5, "*For I was born a sinner*". You don't have to teach a two-year-old to hit her friend upside the head when she wants to take her toy—it comes naturally because she has a sinful nature, just like the rest of us.

Even though you and I want to do the right thing, there always seems to be something pulling at us that makes us want to do the wrong thing instead.

> **POSSIBLE ILLUSTRATION:**
>
> Pick 3 volunteers
>
> One girl stands in the middle, and each of the other girls takes one of her arms. Say this:
>
> "The girl on the right represents our sinful nature. (Have her give her best "sinful nature" face.) Then the girl on the left represents our desire to do the right thing. (Have her make her best "good girl" face.)
>
> "Let's say her Mom has asked her to pick up her room, but she REALLY wants to finish watching a show on TV. Her Mom keeps asking her—and telling her—to go right now.
>
> "(Have each girl pull on her arm—gently, of course!—back and forth like each is trying to get her to go their way.) She wants to do the right thing, but something inside her keeps telling her to stay right there on the couch, even though she KNOWS she should get up and help. She starts to get up (pull to the good side) but then she decides she will just wait another minute (pull to the bad side).
>
> Her Mom reminds her again, and she snaps back into reality and jumps up to go (pull to the good side)... and then she sees something funny on the screen and sits back down again (pull to the bad side.) Back and forth, back and forth. She knows what she should do, but she just can't seem to do it!

Paul talks about this very thing in Romans 7:

> *And I know that nothing good lives in me, that is, in my sinful nature. I want to do what is right, but I can't. I want to do what is good, but I don't. I don't want to do what is wrong, but I do it anyway (vs. 18–19).*

Polka Dot Girls ❀ Self-Control

week 1

Can anyone relate to our buddy, Paul? He's describing in detail what it means to not have self-control. Deep in his heart, he wants to do the right things, but he feels the war within him. The things he wants to do, he doesn't do. And the things he doesn't want to do, he finds himself doing. Let's keep reading…

But if I do what I don't want to do, I am not really the one doing wrong; it is sin living in me that does it. I have discovered this principle of life—that when I want to do what is right, I inevitably do what is wrong (vs. 20–21).

Paul is telling us that no matter how hard we really want to do the right thing, the sinful nature inside of us will always be fighting against us. Now does this mean that whenever you do something wrong, you can simply say, "Sorry Mom, my sinful nature made me do it"? You can give it a try, but I don't think she's going to buy it!

BUT, it can still be helpful to realize that there's really something going on inside us that makes it hard to do the right thing.

I used to get pretty discouraged and upset with myself when I couldn't make my New Year's Resolution happen. I would beat myself up and wonder what was wrong with me. Paul shows this same frustration in Romans 7 when he says,

Oh what a miserable person I am! Who will free me from this life that is dominated by sin and death? (vs. 24).

So what are we to do about this? How can we learn to do the right thing at the right time? How do we learn the art of self-control?

➡ 1. Ask God to Help.

If you were to read a book on self-control, you would find a lot of talk about willpower and motivation and working really hard to meet your goal. I'm not saying those things are bad—you're definitely going to need a healthy dose of each of those things in order to live a self-controlled life. But if we believe what Paul is saying in Romans, then we should realize that not having self-control is a spiritual problem. There's sin at work in our hearts, which causes us to struggle with doing the right thing.

Bottom line: You can't do it by yourself.

Without Jesus, we're powerless against sin. Our sinful nature is strong, and there's only one thing stronger: Jesus.

Romans 7:24–25 says, "*Who will free me from this life that is dominated by sin and death? Thank God! The answer is in Jesus Christ our Lord.*"

Yes, your sinful nature is strong. But Jesus is stronger! Yes, it can be hard to fight to do the right thing. But Jesus has promised to help you!

When we ask Jesus to come into our lives, He comes and lives inside of us and helps us do the right thing. He has broken the power of sin in us, and if we choose to let Him, He will give us the strength to do the right thing. His Holy Spirit fills us with power, and we're suddenly able to conquer those areas of our lives that we used to think would always beat us. Jesus is stronger than our sinful nature.

As we talk about self-control in this Bible study, I know there will be times where you feel discouraged and think you just have to **TRY** harder. I want to encourage you, in those moments when you feel weak, remember that Jesus is the source of your strength! Ask Him to help you and believe that He will help you control yourself.

⇨ 2. Train Yourself to be Disciplined.

First Corinthians 9:27 says, "*I discipline my body like an athlete, training it to do what it should.*"

Callie loves to play soccer. She's been playing since she was really little, and every year she gets better and better. But this year, she has a new coach who's pushing her harder than anyone ever has before. During practice, he makes the

week 1

team do drills over and over again. They would practice kicking the ball back and forth, back and forth over and over and over again until Callie wanted to scream.

Finally, one day she asked her coach, "Why do we practice the same drill so much?" He said, "We practice over and over again because during the game, it's so easy to become distracted by the crowd, the other team, and even your own emotions. When you practice the same drill over and over again, your mind will automatically know what to do in the heat of the moment because you have trained yourself. It prepares you for the moment of truth when you need to rely on what you've learned, even when it's challenging."

It's the same way with EVERYTHING in life! The more you practice, the easier it is to remember what you're supposed to do. The more you practice your math flashcards, the easier it is to remember your math facts. The more you practice your piano lesson, the easier it is for you to play through the songs you're learning. The more you practice riding that new skateboard, the less likely you are to fall on your booty!

Training ourselves to be self-controlled is so important. That means that we have to make ourselves do the right thing even when we don't feel like it. We choose to get up off the couch and help our mom with the dishes the first time she asks us. We pick the apple off the snack cart even though we REALLY want the cookie because we know the apple is better for us. We tell our sinful nature "NO" and control ourselves!

You know why it's so important to train yourself to be self-controlled in the everyday things?

Because the self-control I use when I help my mom with the dishes is the same self-control I use when I say "no" to the friend asking me to cheat on a test. The self-control I use when I pick an apple is the same self-control I use when I don't steal that video game I really, really want but can't afford. The self-control that makes us choose the right thing with the little stuff is the same self-control that will help us choose the right thing with the big stuff.

1 Timothy 4:8 says, "*Physical training is good, but training for godliness is much better, promising benefits in this life and*

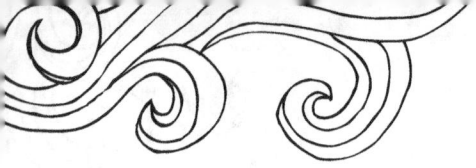

in the life to come." I love how the Message version translates this same verse: *"Exercise daily in God—no spiritual flabbiness, please! Workouts in the gymnasium are useful, but a disciplined life in God is far more so, making you fit both today and forever."*

You need to train yourself to be self-controlled. Do something to work toward discipline. Practice saying "no" to your sinful nature. Challenge yourself in the small things so you will know how to discipline yourself in the big things.

The bottom line is this: Self-control is simply listening to what God tells you to do—and then doing it.

Pretty simple, right?

Well, it may be simple, but simple doesn't necessarily mean easy. Let's trust God to help us be disciplined and self-controlled in every area of our lives. Jesus has promised to help us, so let's do it!

week 1

Kindergarten and 1st Grade Group Discussion Questions

1. Every year, my New Year's resolution was to not get into trouble. No matter how hard I tried, it seemed like I ended up in trouble anyway. Have you ever had an experience like that—something you decided you were NEVER going to do again and yet did it anyway?

2. Or maybe something you decided you were GOING to do every day like practicing piano or being nice to your brother, and yet you found yourself NOT doing that thing? Share your story with the group.

3. In Romans 7, Paul talks about wanting to do the right thing, but something inside of him pulls at him to do the wrong thing instead. Do you remember what Paul said is pulling at him? *(Answer: our sinful nature)*

4. Romans 7 also tells us that only one thing is stronger than our sinful nature? Do you remember what that is? *(Answer: Jesus!)*

5. Practice saying Romans 7:24–25 together: "*Who will free me from this life that is dominated by sin and death? Thank God! The answer is in Jesus Christ our Lord.*"

6. Why is it so important to practice self-control in the small things? *(Answer: when we practice self-control in the little things, it will help us be self-controlled in the big things!)*

7. What are some ways you can *train* yourself to be more self-controlled?

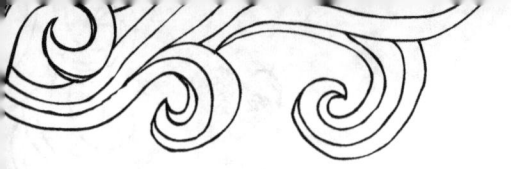

Polka Dot Girls ❖ Self-Control

week 1

2nd and 3rd Grade Group Discussion Questions

1. Every year, my New Year's resolution was to not get into trouble. No matter how hard I tried, it seemed like I ended up in trouble anyway. Have you ever had an experience like that—something you decided you were NEVER going to do again and yet did it anyway?

2. Or maybe something you decided you were GOING to do every day like practicing piano or being nice to your brother, and yet you found yourself NOT doing that thing? Share your story with the group.

3. What is the number one area in your life where you struggle with practicing self-control?

4. In Romans 7, Paul talks about wanting to do the right thing, but something inside of him pulls at him to do the wrong thing instead. Do you remember what Paul said is pulling at him? *(Answer: our sinful nature)*

5. Romans 7 also tells us that only one thing is stronger than our sinful nature? Do you remember what that is? *(Answer: Jesus!)*

6. Practice saying Romans 7:24–25 together: *"Who will free me from this life that is dominated by sin and death? Thank God! The answer is in Jesus Christ our Lord."*

7. Do you really believe God can help you with these areas of your life, or do you feel the weight of doing it on your own? Share your thoughts with the group.

8. Why is it so important to practice self-control in the small things? *(Answer: when we practice self-control in the little things, it will help us be self-controlled in the big things!)*

9. What are some ways you can *train* yourself to be more self-controlled?

Polka Dot Girls ❀ Self-Control

week 1

4th and 5th Grade Group Discussion Questions

1. Every year, my New Year's resolution was to not get into trouble. No matter how hard I tried, it seemed like I ended up in trouble anyway. Have you ever had an experience like that—something you decided you were NEVER going to do again and yet did it anyway?

2. Or maybe something you decided you were GOING to do every day like practicing piano or being nice to your brother, and yet you found yourself NOT doing that thing? Share your story with the group.

3. What is the number one area in your life where you struggle with practicing self-control?

4. In Romans 7, Paul talks about wanting to do the right thing, but something inside of him pulls at him to do the wrong thing instead. Have you ever felt that tug of war in your heart? What are some words that describe how that feels?

5. What is the number one area in your life where you struggle with practicing self-control?

6. Romans 7 also tells us that only one thing is stronger than our sinful nature? Do you remember what that is? *(Answer: Jesus!)*

7. Practice saying Romans 7:24–25 together: *"Who will free me from this life that is dominated by sin and death? Thank God! The answer is in Jesus Christ our Lord."*

8. Do you really believe God can help you with these areas of your life, or do you feel the weight of doing it on your own? Share your thoughts with the group.

9. What are some ways you can let Jesus help you fight your flesh? *(Possible Answers: pray when you're feeling tempted, memorize Scripture and recite them when your flesh is fighting you, remind yourself that Jesus is stronger than your flesh.)*

10. Why is it so important to practice self-control in the small things? *(Answer: when we practice self-control in the little things, it will help us be self-controlled in the big things!)*

11. What are some ways you can *train* yourself to be more self-controlled?

week 1

"Training" Headbands

<u>Supplies Needed:</u>
- White cotton headbands
- Fabric markers
- Optional:
  - Fabric glue
  - Glitter glue
  - Gems

<u>What Should We Do Next?</u>
- Decorate the headbands with fabric markers.
- For added bling, use special jewels and glitter glue.
- Optional: Teachers, write 1 Peter 1:13 on each headband to remind the girls to think clearly and "exercise" self-control.

Parent Partner

Ahhh…self-control. So easy to talk about, and yet exponentially harder to practice. This study was birthed out of a season when God was challenging me regarding the lack of discipline in my life. It seemed like every time I turned around, He was pointing out yet another area where I was stumbling into sin. My lack of control of my time, money, thoughts, tongue, and many other areas were constantly tripping me up.

It wasn't that I didn't KNOW the right thing to do. The problem was that in the moment that really counted, I didn't make myself make the right choice. I didn't eat the apple instead of the cookie. I didn't put back the extra things in my cart that weren't on the list. I didn't stop myself from sharing that juicy piece of gossip. I didn't take control of thoughts that led me to fear, worry, and fret.

Practicing self-control isn't easy, but the good news is that God has promised to help us! This week in POLKA DOT GIRLS, we focused on Romans 7. Paul laments his own struggle to do what he wants to do and stop doing what he doesn't want to do. As his frustration climaxes, he cries out, "Who will free me from this life that is dominated by sin and death? Thank God! The answer is in Jesus Christ our Lord."

We encouraged the girls to recognize that there is something at work in all of us that pulls us toward the wrong things. In those pivotal moments of decision, we can run to Jesus and ask Him to help us do the right thing.

We also talked about training ourselves to be self-controlled. It's not enough to just want to do the right thing—we have to actually practice making the right choices in those pivotal moments. And practicing self-control in the little things will teach us how to make good choices in the big things in life.

I invite you to be really involved with your daughter as she does this study. Gently remind her of the things she's working on, and encourage her when you see her disciplining herself and practicing self-control.

(If you're interested, the adult version of this study, *Undisciplined*, is available at kristiekerr.com.)

week 1

Kindergarten and 1st Grade Take Home Activity Sheet

God wants to help you control yourself. One of the ways God wants you to grow in self-control is by spending time praying and reading the Bible every day.

Draw a picture of yourself reading the Bible.

Polka Dot Girls ❀ Self-Control

week 1

2nd and 3rd Grade Take Home Activity Sheet

In Romans 7, Paul talks about wanting to do the right thing, but something inside of him pulls at him to do the wrong thing instead. Jesus wants us to have self-control. It's much better to think before you act.

Find your way through the maze. Remember to think before you act!

Polka Dot Girls ❀ Self-Control

week 1

4th and 5th Grade Take Home Activity Sheet

You need to *train* yourself to be self-controlled. Next to each letter, list something you can do to work toward self-discipline. **Remember:** Challenge yourself in the small things so you will know how to discipline yourself in the big things.

Example: S - Scripture memorization

S _____

E _____

L _____

F _____

C _____

O _____

N _____

T _____

R _____

O _____

L _____

In Romans 7, Paul describes in detail what it means to not have self-control. Deep in his heart, he wants to do the right things, but he feels the war within himself. The things he wants to do, he doesn't do. And the things he doesn't want to do, he finds himself doing.

Read Romans 7:15–25 in your Bible, and fill in the missing words in the verses below (all verses NIV).

v. 15 *I do not _____ what I do. For what I want to do I do not do, but what I hate I do.*

v. 16 *And if I do what I do not _____ to do, I agree that the law is good.*

v. 17 *As it is, it is no longer I myself who do it, but it is _____ living in me.*

v. 18 *For I know that _____ itself does not dwell in me, that is, in my sinful nature. For I have the desire to do what is good, but I cannot carry it out.*

v. 19 *For I do not do the good I want to do, but the _____ I do not want to do—this I keep on doing.*

v. 20 *Now if I do what I do not want to do, it is no longer I who do it, but it is sin _____ in me that does it.*

v. 21 *I find this _____ at work: Although I want to do good, evil is right there with me.*

v. 22 *For in my inner being I delight in _____ law;*

v. 23 *But I see another law at work in me, waging war against the law of my mind and making me a _____ of the law of sin at work within me.*

v. 24 *What a wretched man I am! Who will _____ me from this body that is subject to death?*

v. 25 *Thanks be to God, who _____ me through Jesus Christ our Lord! So then, I myself in my mind am a slave to God's law, but in my sinful nature a slave to the law of sin.*

Word List:

Understand	Living	Evil	Want
Law	Sin	Save	God's
Good	Prisoner	Deliver	

Polka Dot Girls ❀ Self-Control

Self-Control

week 2

Good Fruit / Bad Fruit

WHAT'S THE POINT?
I NEED TO PUSH DOWN MY FLESH AND FILL UP WITH THE HOLY SPIRIT!

theme verse

So I say, let the Holy Spirit guide your lives. Then you won't be doing what your sinful nature craves.

Galatians 5:16

related bible story

Galatians 5:16–26

❋ Large Group Lesson ❋

"I HATE cleaning my room!"

Hannah was stomping around her room, throwing things into her closet and muttering under her breath. All her friends were outside enjoying the sunshine while she sat indoors picking up clothes off the floor.

"It's not fair," she said to herself. "All my friends get to do whatever they want. Why does my mom always make me do what SHE wants me to do? I just want to be able to do what I want to do!"

Have you ever had that happen to you? You REALLY want to play outside with your friends, but your parents make you do chores first? Or you REALLY want to have

free time in class, but your teacher makes you do an extra assignment first? Or maybe you really want to play a certain game, but it's your friend's turn to choose and you have to play what she wants instead?

We can probably all remember a time when we didn't get what we wanted. It can be pretty frustrating.

Imagine what it would be like if you could do whatever you wanted ALL the time! Chocolate ice cream for breakfast, lunch, and dinner. Recess for four hours a day. No homework. No chores. As much TV and computer time as you want—whenever you want it.

Sounds pretty good, doesn't it?

Well, it does sound good at first, but what happens when your stomach hurts and you get a toothache from only eating chocolate ice cream? And what happens when you grow up and you don't know how to read or do math because you had recess all day at school instead of learning the things you needed to learn? And what happens when you NEVER clean your room and suddenly you can't find any clean clothes to wear to school and your room starts to smell really bad because of all the stinky socks stuck in the corner? That doesn't sound like much fun either.

Sometimes we think of freedom as being able to do whatever we want. We think we should only have to do the things that are fun! We think we should be able to do things whenever we want to—instead of when our teacher or parents want us to do things. We try and avoid things that are hard and not so fun. But that isn't the way life works. Most of life is made up of doing the things that we SHOULD do, not the things we WANT to do.

You may not feel like cleaning your room, but you know it's the right thing to do. You may not feel like doing your homework, but you do it because you know it's important to learn things. You may not feel like taking turns with your friends, but you do it because you know a good friend takes turns.

One of the greatest ways that we can practice self-control is by doing the things we may not WANT to do, but they're the right things to do.

Polka Dot Girls ❖ Self-Control

week 2

Hannah didn't WANT to pick up her room, but when she choose to obey her parents and do what they asked, she was choosing what was better. She was showing honor to her parents. She was being responsible by taking care of the things she owned. She was being a good example to her friends by doing the right thing. More important than all these things, something happened inside Hannah when she decided to do the right thing, even when she didn't feel like it.

You see, something happens in us when we put aside our own feelings and do what we SHOULD do, even when we don't WANT to.

The Bible talks a lot about our FLESH. What in the world does "flesh" mean? Well, it's the thing inside of us that makes us only think about ourselves and what we want. It's part of the "sinful nature" we talked about last week. It's the little voice inside your head that says, "You should always get what you want." It whispers, "You shouldn't have to do anything you don't want to do." The flesh is all about me, me, me. Making ME happy. Making sure I always get to do what I want.

Ick. Our flesh is pretty yucky.

Jesus tells us over and over again that we should not let our flesh be the boss of us. We should think of others before ourselves. We should do the right thing even if it's not easy. Our flesh wants to lead us down one path, but God's path is way better!

So, how do we fight this flesh thing? How do we overcome that voice that tells us to only do what we want instead of what's right?

There's a magic formula! Ready?

We PUSH down the FLESH and FILL UP with the Spirit!

Teacher Note: As you talk through these points, use these hand gestures for emphasis and have the girls do them with you. Take both hands and make a downward motion when you say "Push down our flesh" and then do the reverse action—raising both hands back up while you say "Fill up with the Spirit."

Practice these three or four times before you explain the following points.

→ 1. Push Down our Flesh.

Galatians 5:16 says, *"So I say, let the Holy Spirit guide your lives. Then you won't be doing what your sinful nature craves."*

Remember last week when we talked about the two sides pulling at us? The tug of war to do the right thing verses the tug of war to do the wrong thing? That's what this verse is talking about. Good and evil are at WAR inside us!

We have to FIGHT hard to help the good side win. And the more the good side wins, the stronger it becomes.

Having self-control means you push down your flesh with everything in you. You tell your mind and body and actions "NO!"

> **ILLUSTRATION:**
>
> (Take an empty garbage can or other container. Fill it with pieces of crumpled up newspaper.)
>
> "Take a look at this garbage can. It is FULL of newspaper. Just like you and I can be FULL of our FLESH. But we don't have to let our flesh be the boss of us. We can push it down!"
>
> (Push down the newspaper with your hand or foot, and maybe let the kids take a turn pushing down the paper too!)
>
> "When we push down our flesh, we make room for the Holy Spirit to fill us up instead!"

Polka Dot Girls ❀ Self-Control

When your flesh tells you to take that cookie even though your Mom told you not to, you push down your flesh and say, "NO COOKIE FOR YOU!" When your flesh tells you to share that secret about a friend that you promised you wouldn't share, you push down your flesh and say, "NO! I'M NOT GOING TO TELL THAT SECRET!" When your flesh tells you to cheat on the test so you can get a better grade, you push down your flesh and say, "NO! I'M NOT GOING TO DO SOMETHING I KNOW IS WRONG!"

First Corinthians 9:27 says, "*I keep my body under control and make it my slave …*" (CEV). Another version says, "*It is my own body I fight to make it do what I want.*" (ERV) Sometimes the thing we're fighting is our very own body. Sometimes I have to smack myself upside the head and say, "No! I will not listen to you! I will not let you be the boss of me!"

Push down your flesh. Don't let it bully you into doing something you know is wrong.

So, we push down then flesh, and then we…

⇒ 2. Fill up with Spirit.

Micah 3:8 says, *"But me—I'm filled with God's power…"* (MSG). And Acts 1:8 says, *"But you will receive power when the Holy Spirit comes upon you".*

When you push down that gross, yucky flesh, you make room for God's awesome and amazing power to fill you up! The Holy Spirit gives you the POWER to fight your flesh and have self-control!

Austin was feeling super nervous about going to school. Every morning he would begin walking toward his school and his mind would start picturing every possible bad thing that could ever happen. He worried that he would drop his tray at lunch. He wondered if his teacher would call on him when he didn't know the answer. He thought about how embarrassed he would be if he didn't have anyone to play with at recess. The more he thought about it, the more anxious and afraid he would get. His thoughts kept coming faster and faster until his heart was beating fast and he thought he might throw up.

But he remembered that he didn't have to let his thoughts boss him around, so the next time a bad thought came into his head, he pushed down his flesh and told it to go away. Over and over again, he knocked those thoughts right out of his head and told them to go away.

Austin realized that, not only did he need to get the bad thoughts out, he needed to fill up with good thoughts. He asked the Holy Spirit to come and fill his thoughts with good things instead. He prayed for the Holy Spirit's power to give him strength to fight his flesh. He remembered a verse his mom taught him that said, *"For I can do everything through Christ who gives me strength"* (Philippians 4:13), and he started saying it over and over again.

He pushed those bad thoughts out and filled his mind with the power of the Holy Spirit. Every time he pushed down the flesh, he filled the space with a reminder that God was with him and he could do anything with God's help!

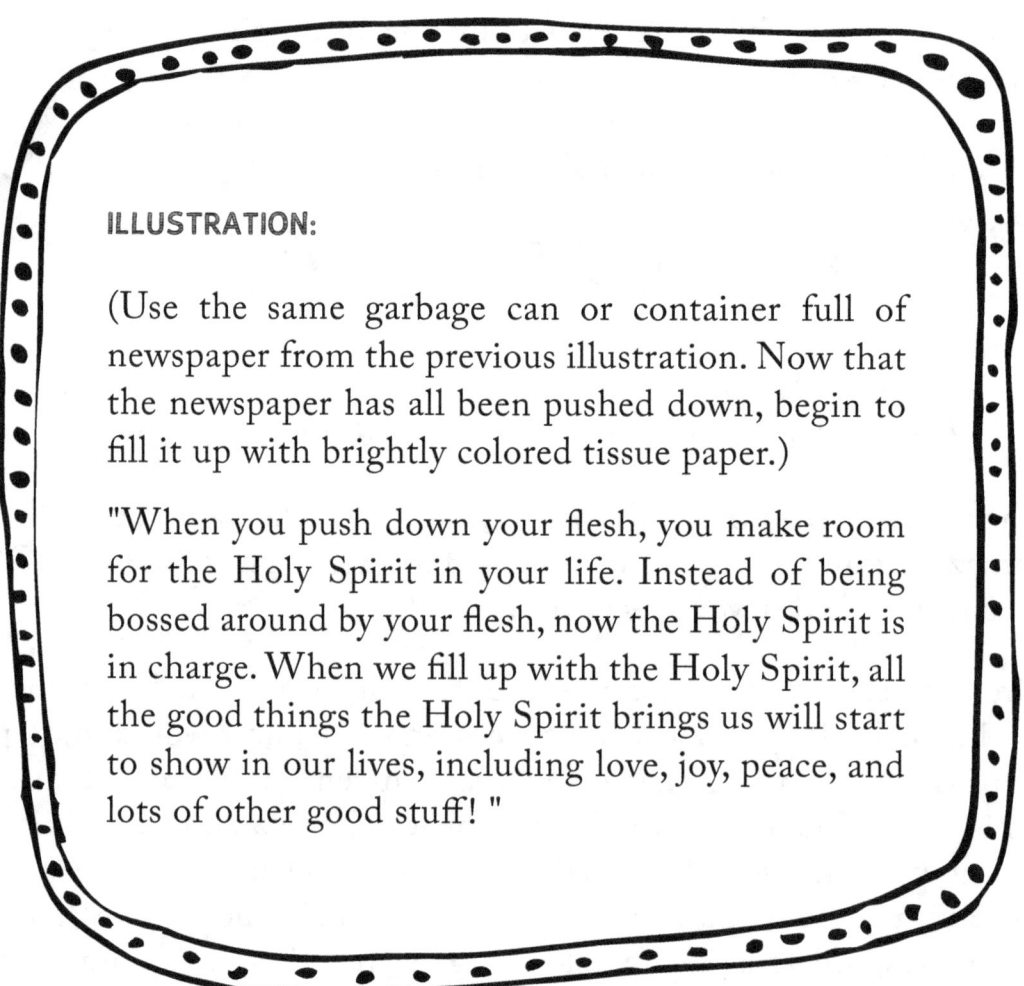

ILLUSTRATION:

(Use the same garbage can or container full of newspaper from the previous illustration. Now that the newspaper has all been pushed down, begin to fill it up with brightly colored tissue paper.)

"When you push down your flesh, you make room for the Holy Spirit in your life. Instead of being bossed around by your flesh, now the Holy Spirit is in charge. When we fill up with the Holy Spirit, all the good things the Holy Spirit brings us will start to show in our lives, including love, joy, peace, and lots of other good stuff!"

The Holy Spirit will fill you with the power to overcome your flesh. He will fight it for you. When you ask Him to help you, His strength comes into you and gives you SUPERNATURAL power to practice self-control.

So, we push down our flesh, we fill up with the Spirit, and then we…

⇨ 3. Grow Some Fruit.

What kind of tree grows an apple? What kind of tree grows an orange? What kind of tree grows a lemon?

Of course an apple tree grows apples. An orange tree grows oranges. And a lemon tree grows lemons. You can tell what kind of tree it is by the kind of fruit it produces. It even says this in the Bible. Luke 6:44 says, *"A tree is identified by its fruit."*

It's the same way with our lives. The Bible says that if we really love Jesus and we're following Him, we'll see certain kinds of fruit in our lives. Galatians 5:22 says, *"But the Holy Spirit produces this kind of fruit in our lives: love, joy, peace, patience, kindness, goodness, faithfulness, gentleness, and self-control."*

If our lives belong to Jesus, the "fruit" of our lives—the things other people notice about us—should be love, joy, peace, and all the other fruits of the Spirit …including self-control!

If we push down our flesh and we fill up with the Spirit, then we'll see more and more of these things in our lives. If I'm filling myself with the Spirit, I'll be a more loving person. If I'm filling myself with the Spirit, I'll be a more patient person. If I'm filling myself with the Spirit, I'll have more self-control.

The reverse is also true, isn't it? If you're not very loving, you need more of the Spirit. If you're not very patient, you need more of the Spirit. And if your life isn't demonstrating self-control, you need more of the Spirit.

If our fruit shows a lack of peace, we need less of the flesh and more of the Spirit. If our fruit shows a lack of gentleness—we're harsh and snappy and unkind—we need less of our flesh and more of the Spirit. And if we find ourselves struggling to be disciplined, we need less of the flesh and more of the Spirit.

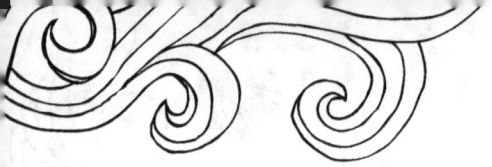

What is the secret to discipline? Less of the flesh and more, more, more of Jesus.

He is the answer. He is where we go to deal with our lack of discipline.

Push down the flesh, fill up with more of the Spirit, and grow good fruit.

week 2

Kindergarten and 1st Grade Group Discussion Questions

1. Share about a time you really, really, really wanted to do something and your mom or dad said you couldn't

2. What is your flesh? (*Answer: It's the part of us that wants whatever it wants whenever it wants it.*)

3. How do you push down the flesh? (*Answer: Tell your body who's boss, tell yourself NO, and do what's right even if you don't want to.*)

4. After you push down the flesh, what do you do? (*Answer: Fill up with the Spirit.*)

5. What does the Holy Spirit do when you ask Him to fill you up? (*Answer: He gives you power to overcome your flesh.*)

6. What kind of fruit does the Holy Spirit produce in us? (*Answer: Love, joy, peace, patience, kindness, goodness, faithfulness, gentleness, self-control.*)

Polka Dot Girls ❀ Self-Control

week 2

2nd and 3rd Grade Group Discussion Questions

1. Share about a time you really, really, really wanted to do something and your mom or dad said you couldn't

2. If you could eat anything you wanted for every single meal for the rest of your life, what would it be?

3. Do you think it would be good for you to have that thing for every meal? Why or why not?

4. What is your flesh? (*Answer: It's the part of us that wants whatever it wants whenever it wants it.*)

5. How do you push down the flesh? (*Answer: Tell your body who's boss, tell yourself NO, and do what's right even if you don't want to.*)

6. After you push down the flesh, what do you do? (*Answer: Fill up with the Spirit.*)

7. What does the Holy Spirit do when you ask Him to fill you up? (*Answer: He gives you power to overcome your flesh.*)

8. What kind of fruit does the Holy Spirit produce in us? (*Answer: Love, joy, peace, patience, kindness, goodness, faithfulness, gentleness, self-control.*)

9. What kind of fruit do you think is showing the MOST in your life? What kind of fruit is showing the LEAST in your life?

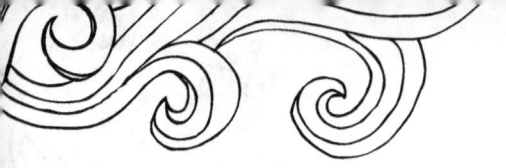

Polka Dot Girls ♣ Self-Control

week 2

4th and 5th Grade Group Discussion Questions

1. Share about a time you really, really, really wanted to do something and your mom or dad said you couldn't

2. If you could eat anything you wanted for every single meal for the rest of your life, what would it be?

3. Do you think it would be good for you to have that thing for every meal? Why or why not?

4. What is your flesh? (*Answer: It's the part of us that wants whatever it wants whenever it wants it.*)

5. How do you push down the flesh? (*Answer: Tell your body who's boss, tell yourself NO, and do what's right even if you don't want to.*)

6. After you push down the flesh, what do you do? (*Answer: Fill up with the Spirit.*)

7. What does the Holy Spirit do when you ask Him to fill you up? (*Answer: He gives you power to overcome your flesh.*)

8. What kind of fruit does the Holy Spirit produce in us? (*Answer: Love, joy, peace, patience, kindness, goodness, faithfulness, gentleness, self-control.*)

9. What kind of fruit do you think is showing the MOST in your life? What would your friends say about you if we asked them this question?

10. What kind of fruit is showing the LEAST in your life? Is there an area where you need to show more kindness? Think of a specific example and share with the group.

Polka Dot Girls ❧ Self-Control

week 2

Fruit Cereal Necklace

<u>Supplies Needed:</u>
- Fruit cereal
- Yarn (one 16" piece per child)
- White cardstock
- Template

<u>Prep:</u>
- Copy template on to the white cardstock.
- Cut card created on the cardstock.
- Cut one piece of yarn per child.

<u>What Should We Do Next?</u>
- Have girls thread fruit cereal onto the yarn.
- When necklace is complete, secure the ends with a knot.
- Color the card with bright, fruity colors!
- Remind each girl that this necklace and card are a reminder to PUSH down their flesh, fill up with the HOLY SPIRIT, and grow FRUIT!

week 2

Parent Partner

We all feel the tug of war between our flesh and the Spirit. We identify with Paul in Romans 7 when he shares the experience of desperately wanting to do the right thing, yet consistently finding choosing to do the very thing he didn't want to do. Our kids are no different. For the most part, they want to do the right thing—to obey us, get their homework done, and refrain from talking back. But they feel that same internal struggle we do, between what we know we SHOULD do and what we find ourselves actually doing.

There's hope for all of us! Even though our flesh tries to pull us to the dark side, we KNOW that the Holy Spirit has the power to help us fight our flesh. This week we taught the girls to fight their flesh by pushing it down when they feel it pulling at them with temptation. And after they push down their flesh, they fill themselves up with the Holy Spirit! They can make space for Him by dying to their flesh and inviting Him to come and fill us up. When they fill up with the Holy Spirit, they can watch the good fruit He promises to grow in them come to life. And if they see good fruit, they can know that the Holy Spirit is at work in their heart! Likewise, when they notice bad fruit popping up (such as a lack of self-control) they can recognize that it's time to push down that flesh again and fill up with more of the Holy Spirit.

Help your child recognize their bad fruit and teach them to rely on the Holy Spirit to grow good fruit in them every day!

Polka Dot Girls ♣ Self-Control

week 2

Kindergarten and 1st Grade Take Home Activity Sheet

Galatians 5:22–23 tells us that the fruit of the Spirit is: love, joy, peace, patience, kindness, goodness, faithfulness, gentleness, and self-control.

Write out the name of each fruit on the tree and then color in the picture!

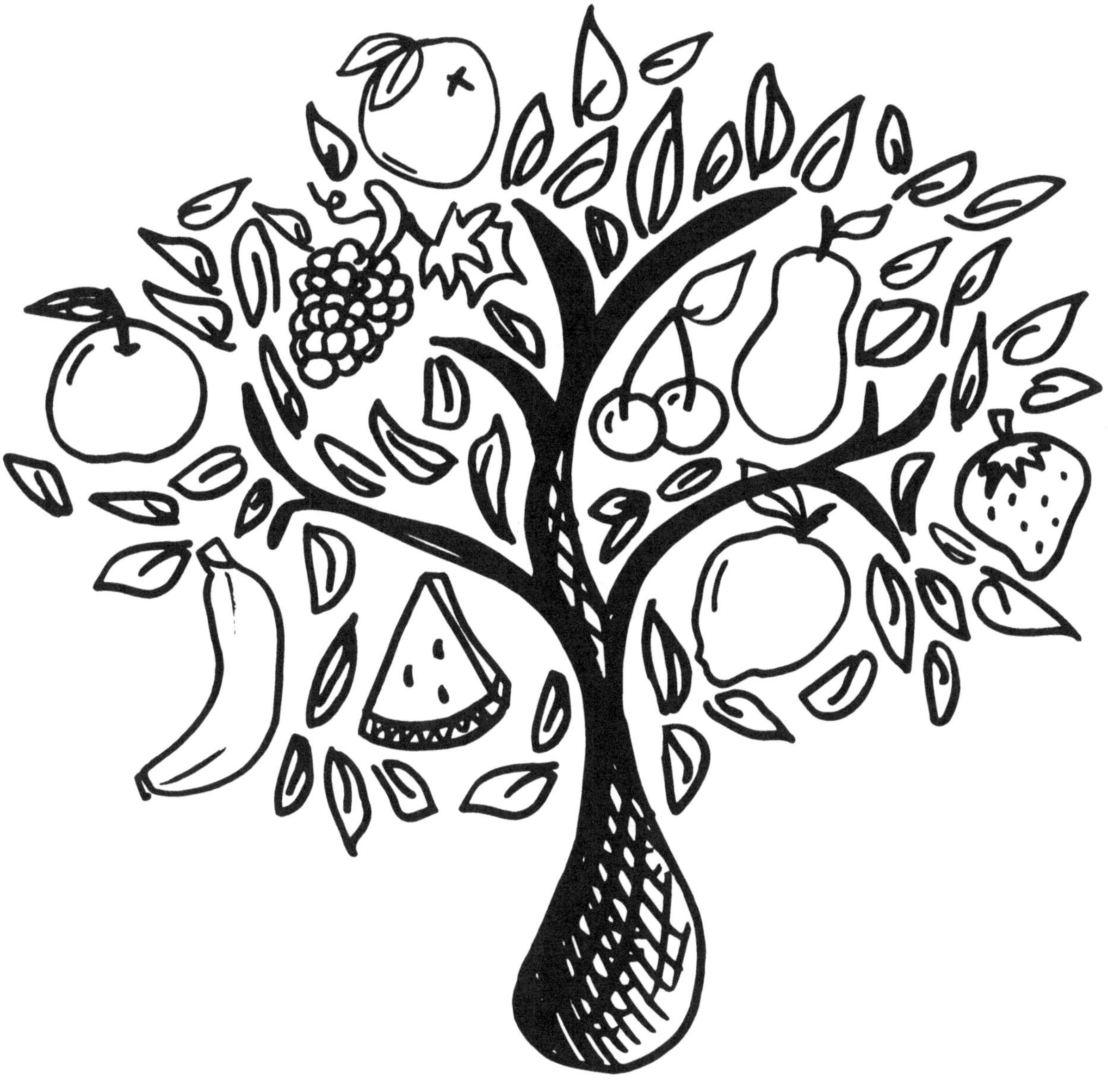

Polka Dot Girls ❖ Self-Control

week 2

2nd and 3rd Grade
Take Home Activity Sheet

Look up Galatians 5:22–23 in your Bible. Write out the nine fruits of the Spirit on the tree and then color the picture.

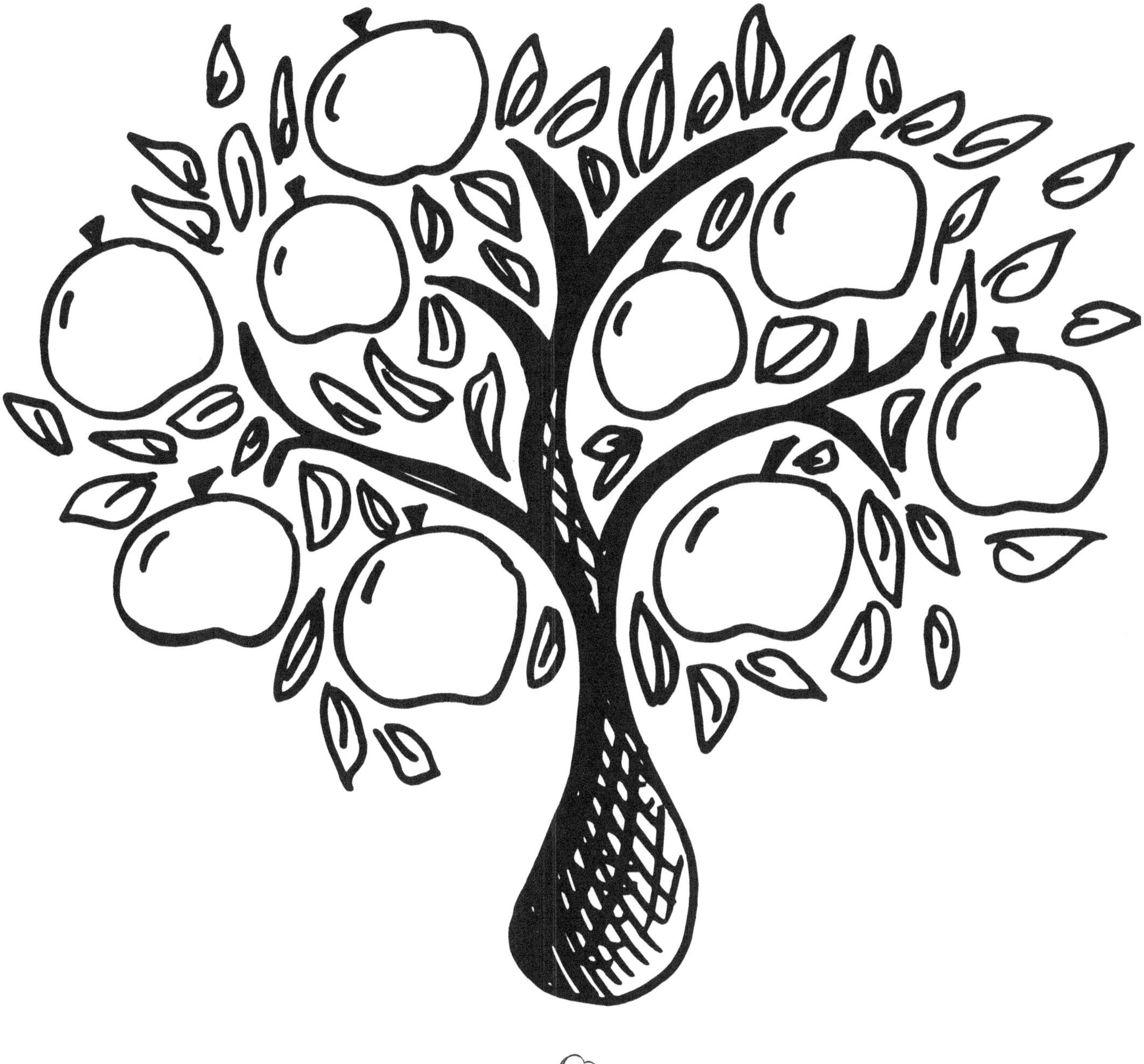

43

Polka Dot Girls ❈ Self-Control

week 2

4th and 5th Grade Take Home Activity Sheet

Look up Galatians 5 in your Bible. Verses 19–21 list 16 bad things that will show up in your life if you're letting your flesh control you. What are they?

1.

2.

3.

4.

5.

6.

7.

8.

9.

10.

11.

12.

13.

14.

15.

16.

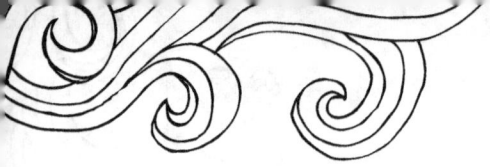

Verse 22 tells us the good fruit that will be present in a life that is controlled by the Spirit. List those nine things here:

1.

2.

3.

4.

5.

6.

7.

8.

9.

Self-Control
week 3

Mind Control

WHAT'S THE POINT?
GOD WANTS YOU TO THINK ABOUT GOOD THINGS, NOT BAD THINGS!

theme verse

*Fix your thoughts on what is true,
and honorable, and right, and pure, and lovely,
and admirable. Think about things
that are excellent and worthy of praise.*

Philippians 4:8

related bible story

Romans 8

❋ Large Group Lesson ❋

Our brains are pretty amazing things. Some people say the average human thinks 70,000 thoughts every single day. That's a lot of thinking!

The Bible tells us Jesus knows EVERY SINGLE THOUGHT WE HAVE! Psalm 94:11 says, *"The Lord knows people's thoughts."* I'm not sure how I feel about that. On one hand, it's so incredible to know God understands every single thing about me without me even saying a word, but on the other hand, I wouldn't say I'm totally proud of each and every thought that crosses my mind. I'm usually happy when I don't act on a negative thought, but the Bible says that if I even think it, He knows it. Yikes! Even more reason to be amazed at God's love for me—He knows everything I think about and still loves me. Crazy!

The Bible encourages us to be careful about the things we think about. God knows how easy it is to think about things we shouldn't. We all have areas of our lives where we allow our thoughts to go places they shouldn't. And sometimes we find our train of thought stuck on a certain pattern of behavior or consumed by a certain way of thinking.

Some of us get stuck always thinking negative thoughts. We can be critical of other people—always putting them down in our minds. We can also be critical of ourselves—saying negative things to ourselves all the time like, "You're so dumb! No one likes you! You're not good at anything!" God doesn't want us to always think negative thoughts.

Maybe you've seen something you shouldn't have seen or done something you shouldn't have done, and now you can't stop thinking about something you know isn't honoring to God.

Some of us get stuck thinking about the past. You can't help but remember and think about things that happened in the past. Maybe you keep thinking about a mistake you made and you replay it over and over again in your mind. It can be so easy to get stuck in the past.

Maybe your mind gets stuck in WORRY mode and your thoughts are consumed by what COULD happen. Your thoughts might even be kind of scary. Your mind seems to always think about the worst possible thing, and you have a hard time stopping it.

So, I have a question for you: why do we let our thoughts focus on such negative things?

Maybe that seems like a trick question. You might be thinking, "What do you mean I 'let' my thoughts be negative?" I don't know about you, but many times I think I don't have any control over the thoughts going through my head. They seem to just happen!

But God tells us that we should CONTROL the thoughts going through our mind. What does it mean to control something? It means you're the BOSS of it. You're in charge and it has to do whatever you tell it to do.

Polka Dot Girls ❀ Self-Control

week 3

Remember last week when we talked about 1 Corinthians 9:27? It says, "*I keep my body under control and make it my slave …*"(CEV). Well, the most important part of your body to keep as your slave is your BRAIN. You can't just let your thoughts go wherever they want to go. Make them your slaves and tell them they have to do whatever you tell them to do!

You know why that's so important? Because your thoughts eventually become your actions. You might think it's not harming anyone else to think bad things, but the truth is that whatever you're thinking about eventually comes out in the way you treat others. Most of all, it will hurt YOU. Proverbs 4:23 says, "*Above all, be careful what you think because your thoughts control your life*" (ERV). The things you think about are important.

Last week, we talked about the fruit of the Spirit: love, joy, peace, patience, kindness, goodness, faithfulness, gentleness, and self-control. This is the good fruit that should be overflowing in our lives. But you know what? Your mind is an easy place to grow BAD fruit.

We aren't very loving because we're filled with unloving thoughts toward other people. We're not filled with joy because our minds are focused on disappointments. Our minds aren't peaceful because we're worried about so many things. We're not patient, kind, good, faithful, or gentle in our thoughts. Instead, we're impatient, rude, harsh, disloyal, and destructive in the things we think about.

So, how can we learn to discipline our thoughts?

⇨ 1. Let the Holy Spirit be the Boss of your Brain.

Who gets to be the boss of your brain? The Holy Spirit! Romans 8:6 says, "*So letting your sinful nature control your mind leads to death. But letting the Spirit control your mind leads to life and peace.*"

We need to push down the flesh that wants to fill our thoughts with negative and sinful things, and instead fill up our minds with the Holy Spirit. Invite the

Holy Spirit into your thoughts. Say, "Holy Spirit, you're the boss of my brain!" When He's in charge, He will fill up your mind with all the good fruit of the Spirit and there won't be room for all that yucky, negative stuff!

The second way you can discipline your THOUGHTS is to

➡ 2. Kick the Habit!

What's a habit? It's something you do all the time without thinking about it. Some people have a habit of biting their nails or chewing with their mouth open. What habits do you have?

We all have habits—and it's no different when it comes to our thought life. It's easy to get in the habit of thinking in a certain way or constantly focusing on a certain topic. And if you want to break ANY habit, you have to work hard at changing your behavior. You have to KICK THE HABIT!

If you're in the habit of thinking of the worst things all the time, you're going to need to change that behavior. Catch yourself focusing on bad stuff. When you realize you're thinking something that isn't good, stop yourself right away and begin to think about good things instead!

Layla had a hard time falling asleep. Every night she would crawl into bed and her mind would begin to go crazy. She would imagine all kinds of scary things. She would imagine there was something in her closet. She would imagine she was lost and couldn't find her mom. Sometimes she even imagined none of her friends would talk to her anymore! She wasn't sure where all these negative thoughts came from, but they sure did bother her.

One day she realized she had gotten in the habit of thinking bad things every night at bedtime. It just got to be the way her brain decided to boss her around at night. So she decided to KICK THE HABIT!

When she got into bed, as soon as the first scary thought popped into her mind, she thought of something funny instead. Or she would repeat a Bible verse her mom had taught her: "*Be strong and courageous! Do not be afraid, for the Lord God is with you wherever you go*" (Joshua 1:9). Every

time her brain tried to take her back to a scary thought, she KICKED that habit right in the teeth and thought of something GOOD instead.

You are in control of what you think about. You have the power to simply stop thinking about things that make you sad, worried, or frustrated. Refuse to focus on those things. Kick that bad habit, and think about good stuff instead! Don't allow your thoughts to go wherever they want to. You can control what you think about.

Psalm 119:95 says, "...*I will quietly keep my mind on Your laws.*" You have the power to keep your mind fixed on the things you want to think about. You have the power to keep your mind fixed on things you shouldn't be thinking about.

And the last way you can discipline your thoughts is to focus on…

⇨ 3. The "W" Plan!

One of my all-time favorite verses in the Bible is Philippians 4:8: *"Finally, brothers and sisters, whatever is true, whatever is noble, whatever is right, whatever is pure, whatever is lovely, whatever is admirable—if anything is excellent or praiseworthy—think about such things."*

Isn't that a great verse? It tells us to think about "WHATEVER" is good! And "WHATEVER" is true! And "WHATEVER" is lovely! So when I'm having a hard time controlling my thoughts, I put up three fingers to make a "W" and start using my "W" plan!

What is the "W" plan?

Well, when a thought comes knocking at the door to my brain, I pretend there's a little peep-hole to look through the door and before I answer it I say, "Are you a WHATEVER thought?" I'm basically asking, "Are you a good thought or a bad thought?" and "Are you a true thought or a lie?" and "Are you a lovely thought or a scary thought?" If it's not a "WHATEVER" thought, I don't open the door! I tell those yucky thoughts to stay outside my brain. I don't want them in there!

Now, we all have times when a bad thought sneaks into our brain. It's just part of being human. But we can decide how long we let those thoughts stick around.

ILLUSTRATION: Sieve vs. Bowl

(Have a pitcher of water, a bowl, and a sieve with a bowl underneath.)

"We all have negative thoughts come into our minds from time to time. Maybe it's a mean thought about a friend. Or maybe it's a scary thought about something bad that might happen. Or maybe it's a thought about something you know doesn't make Jesus happy. Our thoughts are like this pitcher of water."

(Pour the water into the first bowl slowly as you share the next point.)

"But the problem comes when you let that thought just sit in your mind, just like the water is sitting in this bowl. Then that thought just sits there, and stays in your mind and you keep thinking, and thinking, and thinking about it until pretty soon it's affecting your whole life."

(Slowly pour the water into the second bowl through the sieve.)

"BUT you can let your mind be like this sieve. When a thought comes into your mind, you can immediately recognize that it's not a 'WHATEVER' thought and let it roll right out of your brain. This will help you keep your thoughts from getting filled up with things that aren't good for you."

You don't have to LET just any thought just roam around in your brain. If you let the Holy Spirit be the boss, He will help you think about love, joy, peace, and other good things! He will help you KICK THE HABIT of thinking about things that aren't good for you.

Colossians 3:2 says, "*Set your mind on things above, not things of earth*" (NIV). God wants your mind to be a place with lots of good fruit. He doesn't want you feeling sad, scared, angry, or negative all the time. Choose to make your brain a place full of good stuff!

Polka Dot Girls ❀ Self-Control

week 3

Kindergarten and 1st Grade Group Discussion Questions

1. Just for fun, let's try playing a word association game. What's the first thing that pops into your mind when I say each of the following words?
   a. Purple
   b. Smelly
   c. Ice Cream
   d. Breakfast
   e. Bedtime
   f. Happy
   g. Sad
   h. Scared

2. God doesn't want us thinking about negative things, scary things, bad things, or things that make us worried. If you want to, share one thought you've struggled with that made you sad, scared, or nervous.

3. What does the word CONTROL mean? (*Answer: It's what is in charge.*) What does it mean to let the Holy Spirit control your thoughts?

4. When do you struggle most with your thoughts? Is it bedtime? In the morning before school? When you're away from your family? What is one way you could KICK THE HABIT of thinking bad thoughts during those times?

5. What is the "W" plan? What are some true, lovely, pure, excellent, worthy-of-praise things you can think about this week?

Polka Dot Girls ❀ Self-Control

week 3

2nd and 3rd Grade Group Discussion Questions

1. Just for fun, let's try playing a word association game. What's the first thing that pops into your mind when I say each of the following words?
   a. Purple
   b. Smelly
   c. Ice Cream
   d. Breakfast
   e. Bedtime
   f. Happy
   g. Sad
   h. Scared

2. The Bible tells us that God knows every single one of our thoughts. How does that make you feel?

3. God doesn't want us thinking about negative things, scary things, bad things, or things that make us worried. If you want to, share one thought you've struggled with that made you sad, scared, or nervous.

4. John 14:1 says, "*Don't let your heart be troubled.*" That's another way of saying, "Don't LET your mind worry." Have you ever thought about the fact that we have to LET our minds think about negative things? Share your thoughts with the group.

5. Our lesson today said the mind is an easy place to grow bad fruit. What do you think that means? And what happens when our thoughts are negative? (*Possible answer: We began to act like our thoughts. If we're thinking unloving thoughts, soon we're being unloving toward our friends and family.*)

6. What does the word CONTROL mean? (*Answer: It's what is in charge.*) What does it mean to let the Holy Spirit control your thoughts?

7. When do you struggle most with your thoughts? Is it bedtime? In the morning before school? When you're away from your family? What is one way you could KICK THE HABIT of thinking bad thoughts during those times?

8. What is the "W" plan? What are some true, lovely, pure, excellent, worthy-of-praise things you can think about this week?

week 3

4th and 5th Grade Group Discussion Questions

1. Just for fun, let's try playing a word association game. What's the first thing that pops into your mind when I say each of the following words?

    a. Purple

    b. Smelly

    c. Ice Cream

    d. Breakfast

    e. Bedtime

    f. Happy

    g. Sad

    h. Scared

2. The Bible tells us that God knows every single one of our thoughts. How does that make you feel?

3. God doesn't want us thinking about negative things, scary things, bad things, or things that make us worried. If you want to, share one thought you've struggled with that made you sad, scared, or nervous.

4. John 14:1 says, "*Don't let your heart be troubled.*" That's another way of saying, "Don't LET your mind worry." Have you ever thought about the fact that we have to LET our minds think about negative things? Share your thoughts with the group.

5. Our lesson today said the mind is an easy place to grow bad fruit. What do you think that means? And what happens when our thoughts are negative? (*Possible answer: We began to act like our thoughts. If we're thinking unloving thoughts, soon we're being unloving toward our friends and family.*)

6. What does the word CONTROL mean? (*Answer: It's what is in charge.*) What does it mean to let the Holy Spirit control your thoughts?

7. When do you struggle most with your thoughts? Is it bedtime? In the morning before school? When you're away from your family? What is one way you could KICK THE HABIT of thinking bad thoughts during those times?

8. What is the "W" plan? What are some true, lovely, pure, excellent, worthy-of-praise things you can think about this week?

week 3

Set Your Mind on Things Above: Hot Air Balloon!

(Recommended for kindergarten–3rd grade)

Supplies Needed:
- Cardstock—Light Blue, White
- Cupcake liner in any color or pattern (one per girl)
- Jewels, stickers, glitter (optional)
- Scissors
- Markers
- Glue
- Template (one per girl)

Prep:
- Copy the template onto light blue cardstock.

What Should We Do Next?
- Glue your cupcake liner at the top of the lines for the basket.
- Decorate your balloon with jewels, stickers, glitter, etc.
- Cut out clouds from the white cardstock.
- Glue the clouds around the balloon.
- Draw yourself in the basket.

Remind the girls that when they have negative thoughts, they can put them in the basket and send them up to Jesus.

"*Set your mind on the things of Heaven, not of earth.*" –Colossians 3:2

week 3

Paper Lanterns
(Recommended for 4th–5th grade)

Supplies Needed:
- Chinese Lanterns (any size)
- Craft Paint (optional)
- Paint Brushes (optional)
- Jewels or Stickers (optional)
- Twine or Ribbon (approximately 36" per girl)
- Favor Pails (or anything else that works as a small basket)
- Template (one per girl)

Prep:
- Copy the template onto cardstock.

What Should We Do Next?
- Assemble the paper lantern.
- Cut the first piece of twine or ribbon (24").
- Thread one end of the twine or ribbon through a loop at the top of the lantern and secure with a knot.
- Thread the other end of the twine or ribbon through the pail or basket handle.
- Place the basket through the center of the lantern until the "basket" hangs below the lantern. Make sure you hold the other end of the twine or ribbon to ensure the "basket" does not fall.
- Thread the other end of the twine or ribbon through the other loop on the top of the lantern and secure.
- Cut another piece of twine or ribbon (12").

- Tie the additional piece of twine or ribbon to the center of the lantern hook. This piece will serve as a hanger.
- Have the girls write down the things that occupy their mind that are not positive or God honoring on the template. Have the girls put their "thoughts" in the "basket" and give them to God!

I am setting my mind on heaven
and I am going to let go…

I am setting my mind on heaven
and I am going to let go…

I am setting my mind on heaven
and I am going to let go…

I am setting my mind on heaven
and I am going to let go…

I am setting my mind on heaven
and I am going to let go…

I am setting my mind on heaven
and I am going to let go…

Parent Partner

Our minds are a battlefield! We've all experienced the struggle to keep our thoughts focused on the positive, and our daughters are no different. Many of our kids are struggling with worry, anxiety, and fear, and this war is being waged in their minds!

The Bible gives us SO many tools to remind us that our thoughts don't have to be troubled. This week we talked about practicing self-control in the things we think about. We cautioned the girls that our minds are a really easy place to grow bad fruit, but the Holy Spirit has promised to help us control the things we think about. If we ask Him, He'll help us replace our bad thoughts with good thoughts.

We gave the girls three main points to help them keep their thoughts under control. First, we encouraged them to let the Holy Spirit be the boss of their brain. Romans 8:6 tells us that letting the Spirit control our minds will lead to life and peace. When we put the Holy Spirit in charge, He will help us keep our minds thinking the best and not the worst.

Second, we encouraged the girls to "Kick the Habit" of bad thinking. Many of us have become accustomed to thinking negatively about certain things. Or sometimes we have a certain time of day or activity when our thoughts seem to just get away from us. We challenged the girls to "catch themselves" thinking negative things and quickly change those negative thoughts to positive ones.

Last, we taught the girls the "W" plan, which comes from Philippians 4:8: "*Finally, brothers and sisters, whatever is true, whatever is noble, whatever is right, whatever is pure, whatever is lovely, whatever is admirable – if anything is excellent or praiseworthy – think about such things.*" This is a great verse to help us analyze the content of our thought life. When you have a thought, filter it through the "W" list—Is it true? Is it lovely? Is it pure? If it's not, get it out of your brain!

One thing I know for sure is that God does not want His children to be anxious, worried, fearful, negative, or consumed by worst-case scenarios. Encourage your daughter to practice self-control in her thought life, and I believe His peace will come to her heart and mind.

Polka Dot Girls ❀ Self-Control

week 3

Kindergarten and 1st Grade Take Home Activity Sheet

God wants you to think about good things! In the picture below, circle the GOOD things and put an X through the BAD things.

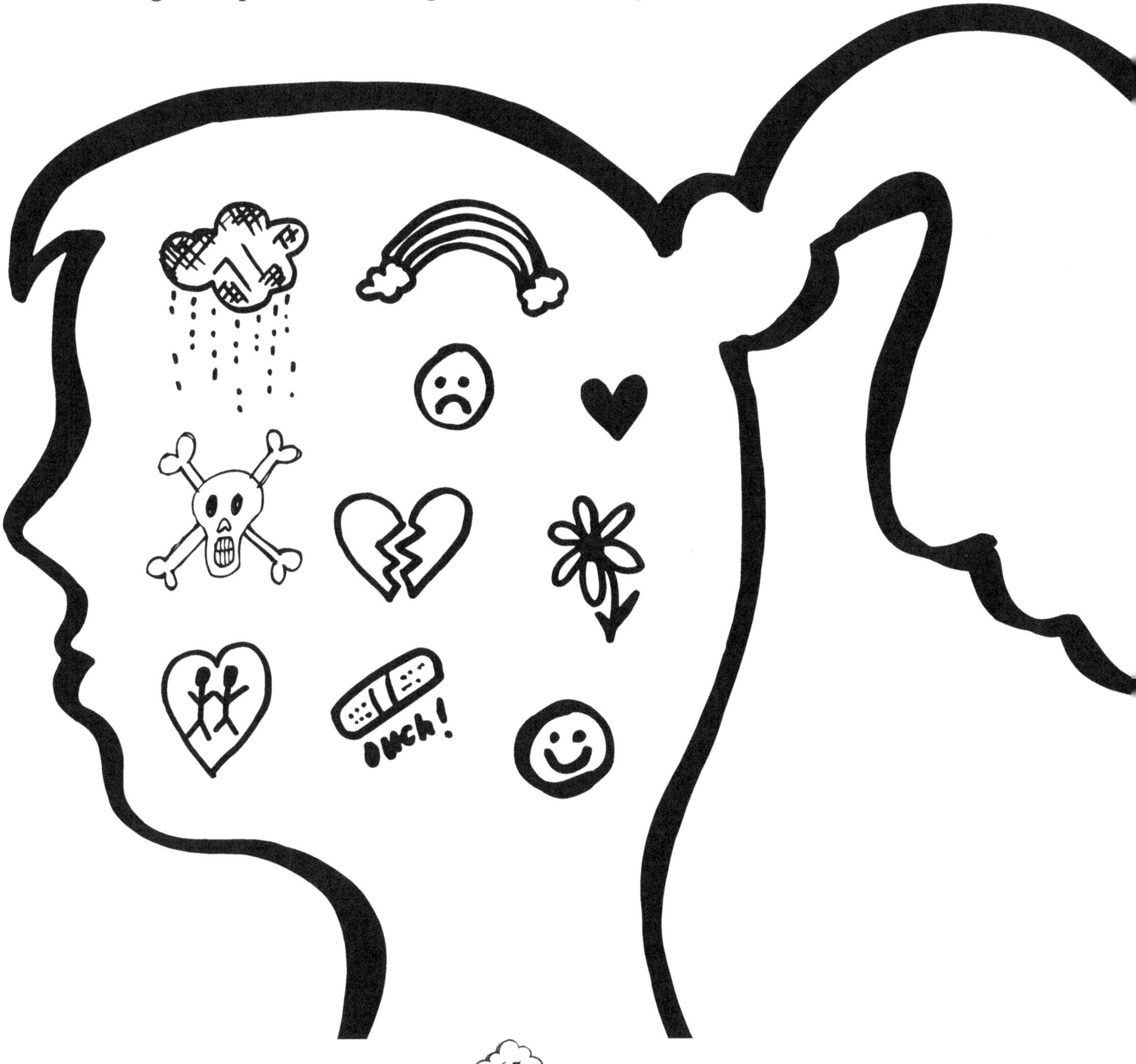

65

God wants us to think about good things! In the verse below, fill in the blank with the word that starts with the same letter!

Word List

True

Honorable

Right

Pure

Lovely

Admirable

Excellent

Worthy

Fix your thoughts on what is T_____, *and* H_____, *and* R_____, *and* P_____, *and* L_____, *and* A_____. *Think about things that are* E_____ *and* W_____ *of praise.*

–Philippians 4:8

Polka Dot Girls ❀ Self-Control

week 3

Now find the words here!

```
Y P W Z W Y C I P D Z X T M A
H U A V A A L Q T R W E N D G
T R M Q Y H Y E S R S B M F S
R E A V J O H O V I U I M T G
O H O W F N A A A O R E W G V
W V X Y W O Y R H A L A F H D
Y F I G F R P T B P A J D P A
Q V Z H O A Z L Z K J N W K Q
D B F M A B E C C U G E S Q D
S X B Y D L T N E L L E C X E
G G W G P E P F L S I V K R G
W Z Y T T J A C G L H Y B L D
Z M W E E H O X R I G H T V B
E M F P R X I N M E V I I A J
P V Q E L C W P B P J J Z G J
```

Word List

True   Pure   Excellent

Honorable   Lovely   Worthy

Right   Admirable

Polka Dot Girls ❀ Self-Control

week 3

2nd and 3rd Grade Take Home Activity Sheet

Look up Proverbs 4:23 in your Bible. Write it out here:

God wants us to be careful with the things we think about. Inside the picture, write some negative things you sometimes think about. Then cross them out and write positive things instead!

Polka Dot Girls ❀ Self-Control

God wants us to think about good things! In the verse below, fill in the blank with the word that starts with the same letter!

Word List

Excellent

Worthy

Pure

Lovely

Honorable

True

Right

Admirable

Fix your thoughts on what is T_____, and H_____, and R_____, and P_____, and L_____, and A_____. Think about things that are E_____ and W_____ of praise.

–Philippians 4:8

Now find the words here!

```
Y P W Z W Y C I P D Z X T M A
H U A V A A L Q T R W E N D G
T R M Q Y H E S R S B M F S
R E A V J O H O V I U I M T G
O H O W F N A A A O R E W G V
W V X Y W O Y R H A L A F H D
Y F I G F R P T B P A J D P A
Q V Z H O A Z L Z K J N W K Q
D B F M A B E C C U G E S Q D
S X B Y D L T N E L L E C X E
G G W G P E P F L S I V K R G
W Z Y T T J A C G L H Y B L D
Z M W E E H O X R I G H T V B
E M F P R X I N M E V I I A J
P V Q E L C W P B P J J Z G J
```

Word List

Admirable

Excellent

Honorable

Lovely

Praise

Pure

Right

True

Worthy

Polka Dot Girls ❀ Self-Control

week 3

4th and 5th Grade
Take Home Activity Sheet

Look up Proverbs 4:23 in your Bible. Write it out here:

God wants us to be careful with the things we think about. Inside the picture, write some negative things you sometimes think about. Then cross them out and write positive things instead!

Polka Dot Girls ❀ Self-Control

week 3

Philippians 4:8 gives us the formula for our "W" test! Look up the verse and fill in the blanks with all the good things we're supposed to think about.

1. _____
2. _____
3. _____
4. _____
5. _____
6. _____
7. _____
8. _____

Now find the words here!

```
Y P W Z W Y C I P D Z X T M A
H U A V A A L Q T R W E N D G
T R M Q Y H E S R S B M F S
R E A V J O H O V I U I M T G
O H O W F N A A A O R E W G V
W V X Y W O Y R H A L A F H D
Y F I G F R P T B P A J D P A
Q V Z H O A Z L Z K H N W K Q
D B F M A B E C C U G E S Q D
S X B Y D L T N E L L E C X E
G G W G P E P F L S I V K R G
W Z Y T T J A C G L H Y B L D
Z M W E E H O X R I G H T V B
E M F P R X I N M E V I I A J
P V Q E L C W P B P J J Z G J
```

Word List

Admirable

Excellent

Honorable

Lovely

Praise

Pure

Right

True

Worthy

Polka Dot Girls ❀ Self-Control

Self-Control
week 4

Watch Your Mouth

WHAT'S THE POINT?

OUR WORDS HAVE POWER, SO WE SHOULD BE CAREFUL WHAT WE SAY.

theme verse

Let the words of my mouth and the thoughts of my heart be pleasing to you O Lord.

Psalm 19:14

related bible passage

James 1:26

❊ Large Group Lesson ❊

Phoebe's little brother was SUCH a pain! He was always coming into her room and messing with her stuff. He spied on her and her friends and told everyone their private conversations. He drove her crazy, and the more angry she got, the more he seemed determined to annoy her.

Her frustration was growing and growing, and she found herself saying really mean things back at him. She knew it wasn't right, but she couldn't seem to stop herself from screaming at him. She kept trying to justify her reaction by telling herself, "He deserves it!" or "If he would leave me alone, I wouldn't have to yell at him!"

But one day she was reading her Bible when she came across James 1:26: *"You might think you are a very religious person. But if your tongue is out of control, you are fooling yourself"* (ERV).

What does it mean for your TONGUE to be out of control? It means you aren't using self-control to make sure the words that come out of your mouth are kind to others and pleasing to God.

Phoebe realized the words she was saying to her brother were not okay. Even though he was wrong, it didn't make her behavior any better. She knew that if she wanted to show God how much she loved Him, she would need to do a better job choosing the words she said to her brother.

The Bible tells us over and over again that our words matter. It's crazy how many verses in the Bible are about watching what you say! Why do you think God took the time to talk to us about this?

Because words are powerful.

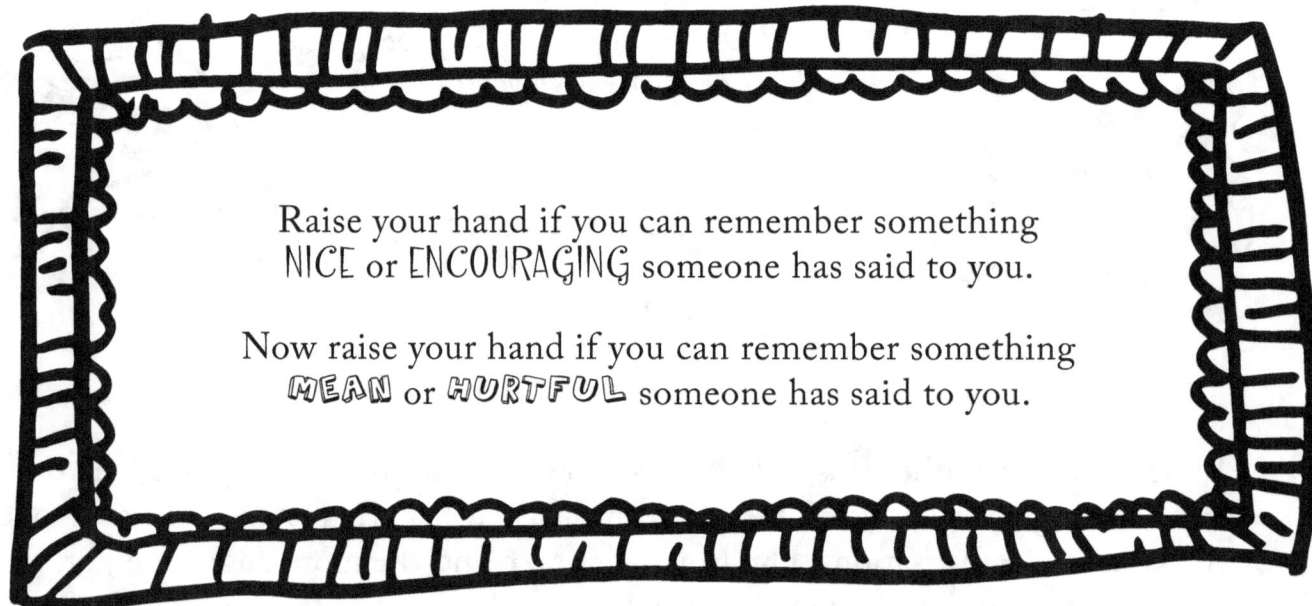

Raise your hand if you can remember something NICE or ENCOURAGING someone has said to you.

Now raise your hand if you can remember something MEAN or HURTFUL someone has said to you.

Think of how you feel when someone says something nice to you. It can change your whole day! It can make you want to try something new. You feel happy, encouraged, and strong when someone says something good.

Now, think of how you feel when someone says something mean or unkind. IT'S THE WORST! When someone says something hurtful, it can make you feel horrible. Those mean words can stick with you for a really, really long time and make you feel bad about yourself.

Polka Dot Girls ❀ Self-Control

week 4

Why? Because our words are powerful.

That's why it's so important to be careful about what we say. It can be so easy to have a thought and then let it slip out of your mouth without ever thinking about what those words might do to another person, but the truth is that our words are a big, big deal. Proverbs 13:3 says, *"Those who control their tongue will have a long life; opening your mouth can ruin everything."*

OBJECT LESSON: Toothpaste tube

Supplies:
- One tube of toothpaste
- Bowl or plate
- Paper towels for cleanup

(Have a volunteer come to the front and ask her to squeeze the toothpaste out of the tube onto the plate. Once she has squeezed out a bunch of the toothpaste, ask her to put the toothpaste back into the tube.)

"Once the toothpaste comes out of the tube, you cannot put it back in. It's the same with our words—once they come out, you can't put them back in again. You can apologize and try and make it right, but once the words come out of your mouth, they go right into the hearts of your family members and friends, and you cannot take them back."

Our words have the power to hurt others, and once you say them, you can't take them back. Even if you're really sorry and apologize, the words you said have already done their damage. This is why it's important to learn to control your tongue and STOP yourself from saying things you shouldn't say.

OBJECT LESSON: Broken pencil

Object Lesson: Broken pencil

(Hold up a pencil and break it in two.)

"When we say words that hurt others, we do damage. We hurt people's feelings, we make others feel bad, and we can disrespect our parents or teachers.

Now, I can say sorry to the pencil. But is it still broken?

I can take tape and try and fix it. I can try and glue it together. But it is still broken.

You and I can do damage to our friends and family if we don't use self-control. Even though we all make mistakes, and God can help us fix it when we hurt our friends, it's much, much easier to choose our words carefully than to try and fix the damage after we say the wrong thing."

So how can we choose good words?

⇒ 1. Clean Words Come from a Clean Heart.

Polka Dot Girls ❀ Self-Control

week 4

Luke 6:45 says, *"A good man says good things. These come from the good that is stored up in his heart. An evil man says evil things. These come from the evil that is stored up in his heart. A person's mouth says everything that is in their heart."* If the words coming out of your mouth are not good words, then you need to look at what's going on in your heart.

> **OBJECT LESSON**
>
> (Take a paper grocery sack, and draw a face on it. Cut out the portion where the mouth should be. Fill the bag with slips of paper that say mean or unkind things.)
>
> Examples:
> - You're stupid.
> - I hate you.
> - You're ugly.
> - I hate what you made for dinner!
> - No one likes you!
> - I DON'T WAAAAANT TO!
> - Did you hear the news about Sally? We shouldn't play with her cause she's so weird.
>
> (Have the kids take turns putting their hands inside the mouth and pulling out a piece of paper and reading what it says.)
>
> "Where are these horrible things coming from? They're coming from what's going on inside! The same is true with us. The things coming out of our mouths are coming from what's inside our hearts."

If you find yourself saying mean, unkind, or inappropriate words, you need to take a good look at your heart. Are you angry inside? Are you scared about something and lashing out at others? Are you feeling bad about yourself, so it seems okay to hurt others, too? Or maybe you've just gotten careless about choosing the right words and you just let your first thought come out instead of practicing self-control?

If you're having a problem with your words, the first thing to do is to look at your heart. Ask Jesus to take away the bad things in your heart that seem to be coming out of your mouth. Pray the prayer King David prayed in Psalm 51:10: *"Create in me a clean heart, O God."* A clean heart is the first step to having clean words.

OPTIONAL OBJECT LESSON:

(Take out all the bad things and fill the bag with good words instead. Have the kids remove the kind words from the mouth and read them out loud.)

Examples:

- You did such a great job!
- I'm sorry.
- I'm frustrated. Can we talk through our problem?
- Can I help?
- I'm so glad you're my friend!
- I'm sorry, but I don't talk about my friends when they aren't here.

Remember that clean words come from a clean heart.

week 4

The second way we can choose good words is to . . .

➪ 2. STOP Talking!

So often, we find ourselves saying things we shouldn't. Many times we KNOW we shouldn't share that secret or yell at our friend or repeat that word you know is inappropriate, but sometimes we just don't make the right choice in the moment. One of the best ways to help control yourself is simply by saying "STOP!"

When you feel yourself starting to say something mean, close your mouth and imagine putting a piece of tape over it. When you start to repeat that juicy piece of gossip about a friend, close your mouth and pretend to lock your lips together and throw away the key. When you're tempted to whine when your mom asks you to set the dinner table, press your lips together **AS TIGHT AS YOU CAN** and repeat inside to yourself, "I will not whine! I will not whine!"

Sometimes the very best thing you can do to control your tongue is just stop talking. There's a verse in the Bible that says, "*A person who talks too much gets into trouble. A wise person learns to be quiet*" (Proverbs 10:19, ERV). A really good way to practice self-control with your words is to simply stop talking when you don't have anything nice to say.

So, clean words come from a clean heart, STOP talking, and lastly…

➪ 3. T.H.I.N.K Before you Speak!

So often, we say whatever pops into our heads. We don't stop to think about the words and how they'll affect the people around us. I learned a really great way to check out my words BEFORE I say them. Here's how it works—before you speak, ask yourself, "Is this …"

True?
Helpful?
Inspiring?
Necessary?
Kind?

Kenzie heard the craziest news about her friend Sara—she had failed a math test and her mom was going to have to come into school to talk to the teacher. At recess, a bunch of the girls came over and began asking her questions about Sara. They were sharing all kinds of rumors and gossip about the situation. Some people were saying she cheated, others were saying she was going to be grounded, and others were just laughing.

Kenzie stopped for a moment and decided to T.H.I.N.K. before she spoke. First of all, many of the things the girls said were NOT TRUE. Secondly, nothing the girls said was HELPFUL. It wasn't helping Sara at all to have her friends talking about her when she wasn't there to defend herself. It also wasn't INSPIRING. This conversation wasn't focusing on good things, it was focusing on bad things. Kenzie also wondered if it was NECESSARY to talk through the issues with these girls. It didn't seem right to talk about what had happened without Sara being there. And lastly, she asked herself if it was KIND to talk to her other friends about something that might be embarrassing to Sara. She realized she would be hurt if the same thing happened to her, so she decided the conversation wasn't KIND.

Once Kenzie went through her T.H.I.N.K. list, she was convinced she shouldn't be having that conversation. She told the other girls that she didn't think it was very nice to talk about this and she turned around and walked away. Although it could have been really easy to just go along with her friends, Kenzie decided to T.H.I.N.K. before she spoke.

Our words are powerful. The things we say can build people up or tear them down. They can make people feel better or make them feel worse. They can honor our parents and teachers, or they can show disrespect. They can be honest, or they can be full of lies. They can be grateful, or they can be whining and complaining.

Colossians 4:6 says, *"Let your conversations always be full of grace and seasoned with salt."* When something is seasoned with salt, it makes people thirsty! When our conversations are filled with grace (kind and good things), people will be thirsty to know more about Jesus. There's nothing I want more than that! So let's choose our words carefully and practice self-control.

Polka Dot Girls ❀ Self-Control

week 4

Kindergarten and 1st Grade Group Discussion Questions

1. Our words are powerful. Think of something encouraging someone has said to you that really made a difference in your life and share it with the group.

2. What did we learn from the tube of toothpaste? Why is it so important to remember?

3. Today we learned that clean words come from a clean heart. What could be going on inside someone's heart to make them say mean words?

4. Think of a moment when the best way to practice self-control is to just STOP TALKING. Share with the group.

5. Do you remember what the T.H.I.N.K. principle is? Let's practice saying it together. "Is it…

    True?

    Helpful?

    Inspiring?

    Necessary?

    Kind?

Polka Dot Girls ❋ Self-Control

week 4

2nd and 3rd Grade Group Discussion Questions

1. Our words are powerful. Think of something encouraging someone has said to you that really made a difference in your life and share it with the group.

2. James 1:26 says, *"You might think you are a very religious person. But if your tongue is out of control, you are fooling yourself"* (ERV). What is a religious person? What does this verse mean?

3. What did we learn from the tube of toothpaste? Why is it so important to remember?

4. Today we learned that clean words come from a clean heart. What could be going on inside someone's heart to make them say mean words?

5. Our words are powerful. We can do damage to our friends and family with our words—just like breaking a pencil. Have you ever had to try and repair a relationship that was broken by words? What was that like

6. Think of a moment when the best way to practice self-control is to just STOP TALKING. Share with the group.

7. Do you remember what the T.H.I.N.K. principle is? Let's practice saying it together. "Is it…

True?

Helpful?

Inspiring?

Necessary?

Kind?

Polka Dot Girls ❊ Self-Control

week 4

4th and 5th Grade Group Discussion Questions

1. Our words are powerful. Think of something encouraging someone has said to you that really made a difference in your life and share it with the group.

2. James 1:26 says, *"You might think you are a very religious person. But if your tongue is out of control, you are fooling yourself"* (ERV). What is a religious person? What does this verse mean?

3. What did we learn from the tube of toothpaste? Why is it so important to remember?

4. Today we learned that clean words come from a clean heart. What could be going on inside someone's heart to make them say mean words?

5. Our words are powerful. We can do damage to our friends and family with our words—just like breaking a pencil. Have you ever had to try and repair a relationship that was broken by words? What was that like

6. Think of a moment when the best way to practice self-control is to just STOP TALKING. Share with the group.

7. Do our words have to be spoken out loud? Where are some other ways we have to be careful how we use our words? (*Possible Answers: social media, texts, etc.*)

8. Do you remember what the T.H.I.N.K. principle is? Let's practice saying it together. "Is it…

>True?
>
>Helpful?
>
>Inspiring?
>
>Necessary?
>
>Kind?

Polka Dot Girls ♣ Self-Control

week 4

Polka Dot Girls T.H.I.N.K. Promise

Supplies Needed:
- T.H.I.N.K template
- White cardstock
- Color crayon/markers
- 12x12" cardstock in a variety of colors
- Scissors
- Glue stick or glue
- Pretty embellishments
- Ribbon (12" per girl)
- Masking tape

Prep:
- Copy the T.H.I.N.K. Promise onto white cardstock.
- Cut the 12x12" cardstock into 9.5x12" sections.
- Cut ribbon (12" per girl).

What Should We Do Next?
- Color the T.H.I.N.K. Promise.
- Mount the Promise onto colored cardstock.
- Decorate your frame with pretty embellishments (buttons, flowers, stickers, glitter, etc.).
- Attach the ribbon to the back of the cardstock with masking tape.
- Hang your T.H.I.N.K. Promise on your wall to remind yourself to think before you speak!

Polka Dot Girls T.H.I.N.K. Promise

"Let the words of my mouth and the thoughts of my heart be pleasing to you O Lord."
–Psalm 19:14

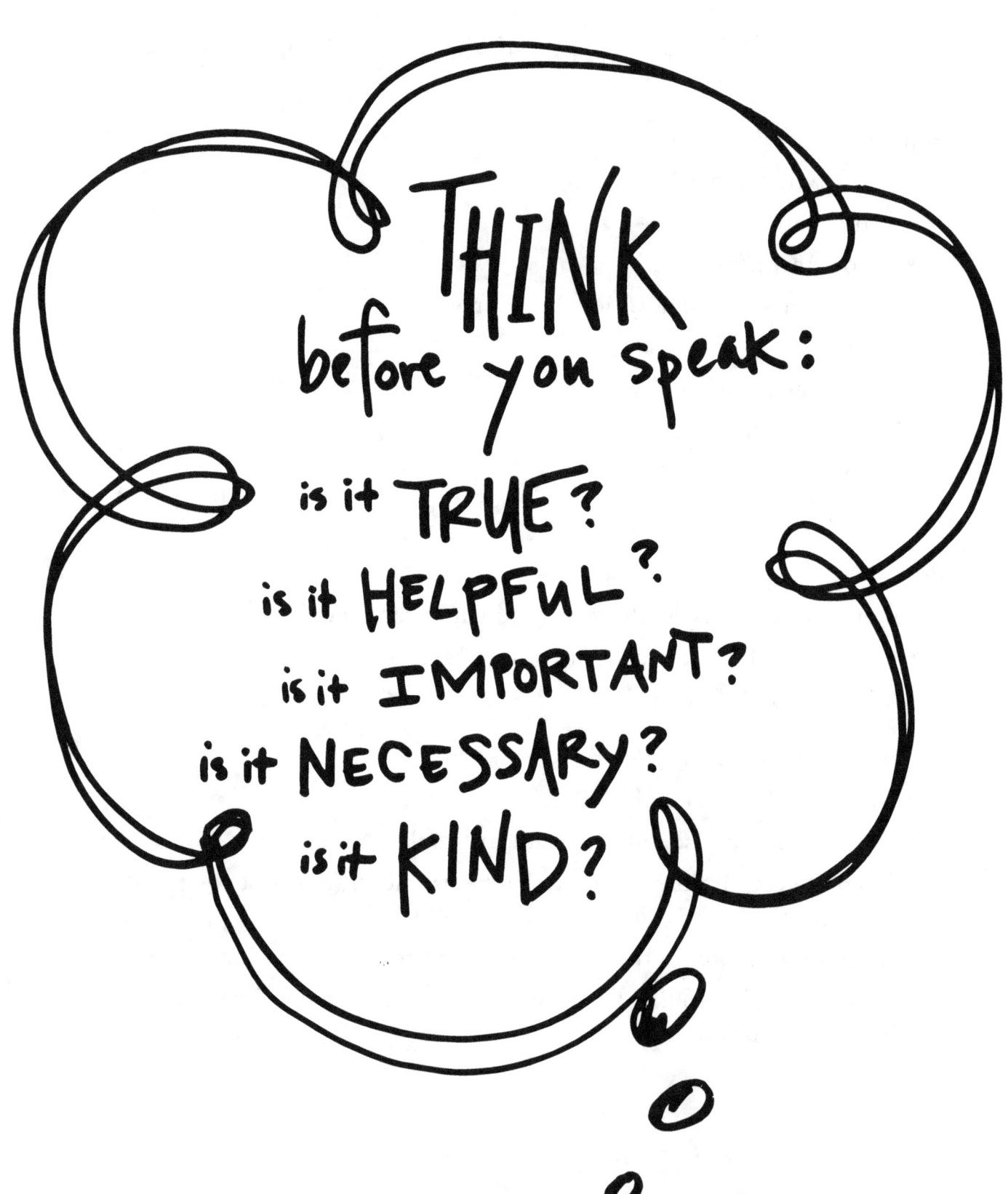

week 4

Parent Partner

We've all heard the saying, "Sticks and stones can break my bones, but words will never hurt me." And we all know how painfully false that statement is! This week we taught the girls that our words are powerful. They have the power to encourage someone and they also have the power to tear someone down and harm them. We showed the girls a tube of toothpaste—once you squeeze all the toothpaste out, you can't put it back inside the tube. Like the toothpaste, once words come out of our mouths, we can't take them back. We need to use self-control BEFORE we speak our words out loud.

Luke 6:45 says, "*A good man says good things. These come from the good that is stored up in his heart. And evil man says evil things. These come from the evil that is stored up in his heart. A person's mouth says everything that is in their heart.*" We reminded the girls that clean words come from a clean heart. If we find ourselves constantly tearing others down, using inappropriate words, or sharing things we should not share, our first job is to look at our hearts and ask God to help us have a clean heart.

Second, we told them that sometimes the very best thing we can do is JUST STOP TALKING! We encouraged them to put their hands over their mouths to keep themselves from blurting out things they will regret later if necessary (a lesson we all could use from time to time)!

Last, we taught the girls the acronym T.H.I.N.K. Before you share something, ask yourself the following questions:

1. Is it True?
2. Is it Helpful?
3. Is it Inspiring?
4. Is it Necessary?
5. Is it Kind?

If you can't answer "yes" to all these questions, perhaps you should keep quiet.

Controlling the tongue is not an easy task, but God has promised to help us if we will do our part by watching the words we use and being careful to only speak life!

week 4

Kindergarten and 1st Grade Take Home Activity Sheet

Ephesians 4:29 says, *"When you talk, don't say anything bad. But say the good things that people need—whatever will help them grow stronger. Then what you say will be a blessing to those who hear you"* (ERV). Write the good words listed below on the flowers to remind yourself that good words help people grow strong, then color in the picture.

Good words:
Nice
Friend
Happy
Help
Smile
Good Job!

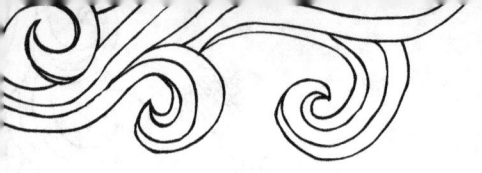

Polka Dot Girls ❀ Self-Control

week 4

2nd and 3rd Grade Take Home Activity Sheet

Ephesians 4:29 says, *"When you talk, don't say anything bad. But say the good things that people need—whatever will help them grow stronger. Then what you say will be a blessing to those who hear you"* (ERV). Write the good words listed below on the flowers to remind yourself that good words help people grow strong, then color in the picture.

Good words:
Nice
Friend
Happy
Help
Smile
Good Job!

Look up Proverbs 12:18 in your Bible and write it out below:

Polka Dot Girls ❀ Self-Control

Use the key to solve the word problem below.

Ephesians 4:29

A	B	D	E	G	H	I	K	L	M	N	O	P	R	S	T	U	V	W	Y
15	5	23	8	16	19	7	6	14	17	10	11	3	1	26	20	4	21	13	24

"WHEN YOU TALK, DON'T
SAY ANYTHING BAD.
BUT SAY THE GOOD
THINGS THAT PEOPLE
NEED — WHATEVER WILL
HELP THEM GROW
STRONGER. THEN WHAT
YOU SAY WILL BE A
BLESSING TO THOSE
WHO HEAR YOU."

Polka Dot Girls ❖ Self-Control

week 4

4th and 5th Grade
Take Home Activity Sheet

Look up the following verses in your Bible and write them below:

Psalm 141:3   Proverbs 18:21   Proverbs 12:14   Proverbs 12: 18

Use the key to solve the word problem below.

Ephesians 4:29

A	B	D	E	G	H	I	K	L	M	N	O	P	R	S	T	U	V	W	Y
15	5	23	8	16	19	7	6	14	17	10	11	3	1	26	20	4	21	13	24

"W H E N   Y O U   T A L K ,   D O N ' T
13 19 8 10   24 11 4   20 15 14 6   23 11 10   20

S A Y   A N Y T H I N G   B A D .
26 15 24   15 10 24 20 19 7 10 16   5 15 23

B U T   S A Y   T H E   G O O D
5 4 20   26 15 24   20 19 8   16 11 11 23

T H I N G S   T H A T   P E O P L E
20 19 7 10 16 26   20 19 15 20   3 8 11 3 14 8

N E E D — W H A T E V E R   W I L L
10 8 8 23   13 19 15 20 8 21 8 1   13 7 14 14

H E L P   T H E M   G R O W
19 8 14 3   20 19 8 17   16 1 11 13

S T R O N G E R .   T H E N   W H A T
26 20 1 11 10 16 8 1   20 19 8 10   13 19 15 20

Y O U   S A Y   W I L L   B E   A
24 11 4   26 15 24   13 7 14 14   5 8   15

B L E S S I N G   T O   T H O S E
5 14 8 26 26 7 10 16   20 11   20 19 11 26 8

W H O   H E A R   Y O U ."
13 19 11   19 8 15 1   24 11 4

Polka Dot Girls ❀ Self-Control

Self-Control
week 5

Money Matters

WHAT'S THE POINT?
EVERYTHING WE HAVE COMES FROM GOD, AND WE NEED TO DO WHATEVER JESUS TELLS US TO DO WITH OUR MONEY AND THINGS.

theme verse

And God will generously provide all you need. Then you will always have everything you need and plenty left over to share with others.
2 Corinthians 9:8

related bible passage
John 6:5–15

❋ Large Group Lesson ❋

Has anyone ever given you money? Maybe you got a five-dollar bill in a birthday card from your grandparents? Or maybe your parents gave you a dollar for doing an extra chore? Or maybe you found a quarter on the ground?

Do you want to hear something really cool? The Bible tells us **GOD** is the one who gives us money. I know that can seem crazy because it seems like our money is given to us by other people. But the truth is, when someone gives you money, they're doing it because God wants them to do it. God is in charge of **ALL** the money in the whole world, and He gives it to us to use for the things He wants us to use it for.

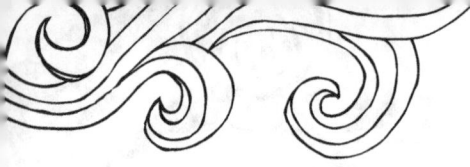

First Chronicles 29:14 says, "*Everything comes from you. We've given back to you only what comes from you.*" And verse 16 of that same chapter says, "*But all of it comes from you. All of it belongs to you*" (NIRV).

God owns all the money in the entire universe, and He gives it to us to use. Another cool verse—Psalm 50:12—says, "*I already own the world and everything in it*" (ERV). Everything in the whole world belongs to God. He's the boss.

One cool thing about God is that He gives us money to buy things. He gives your parents jobs so they can earn money to pay for your house and food. He gives your grandparents money so they can come visit you. He gives YOU money to buy toys, treats, and lots of other things.

It's so important to remember that everything we have belongs to God. That means our money and all our things! When we remember that, it changes the way we take care of what we have.

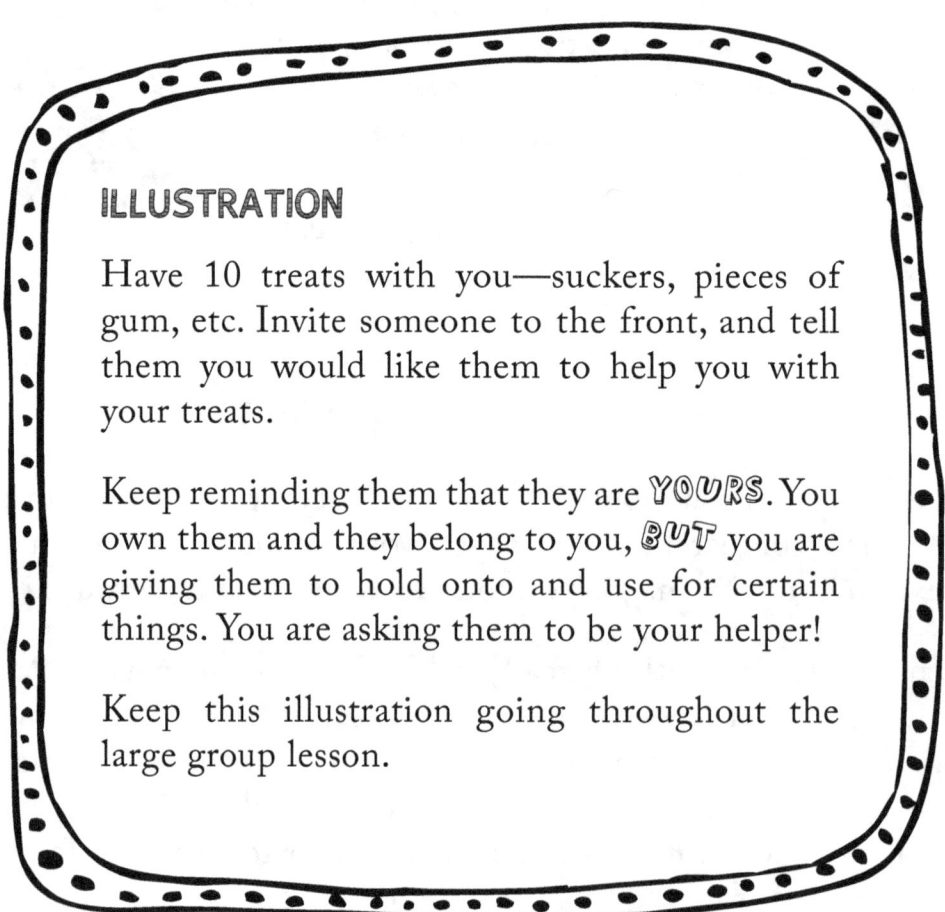

ILLUSTRATION

Have 10 treats with you—suckers, pieces of gum, etc. Invite someone to the front, and tell them you would like them to help you with your treats.

Keep reminding them that they are YOURS. You own them and they belong to you, BUT you are giving them to hold onto and use for certain things. You are asking them to be your helper!

Keep this illustration going throughout the large group lesson.

Polka Dot Girls ❊ Self-Control

week 5

So what does it mean to have self-control with our money and the other things God has given us to take care of? Practicing self-control means we don't do things without thinking—and we make sure we do the things God wants us to do! When it comes to our money, we need to make sure we think about the way God wants us to use the things he's given us to hold.

What are some ways we can have self-control with our money and things?

⇨ 1. Give Back to God What He Asks you to Give.

Sarah saw her mom with a calculator, her computer, and a checkbook. She asked her mom what she was doing, and she said, "I'm paying bills." Sarah was curious, so she asked, "What's the very first bill you pay?" Sarah's mom replied, "Oh, that's easy. The very first check I write is to our church! I know God has provided money for our family, so I make sure I give my very first offering to Him!"

Have you ever heard the word "tithe"? It's a funny word that comes up several times in the Bible. The first place it's mentioned is in Deuteronomy 14:22–23, which says, *"You must set aside a tithe of your crops—one-tenth of all the crops you harvest each year. Bring this tithe to the designated place of worship…"* People would bring the VERY best of their crops and animals to the Temple and give them back to God. They brought ten percent of everything they grew as an offering to God!

ILLUSTRATION

(Refer back to the volunteer with the treat.)

"Tithing means we give ten percent back to God. So using my friend here as an example—since you have 10 items, you would give one back to me!"

(Have the student give you one treat back as a "tithe.")

105

When we tithe, we're reminding ourselves that all our money REALLY belongs to God. It's a way of saying "THANK YOU" for all the things He's provided for us!

Now what that means is that whatever money you and I get, we give ten percent back to God's work. Most people give their tithes to the church they go to. Churches use that money to help tell other people about Jesus. So when you tithe, you're helping the people in your community hear how much Jesus loves them. That's a pretty awesome way to spend your money!

The second way you can practice self-control with your money

➡ 2. Take Care of the Stuff God Gives you.

> **ILLUSTRATION**
>
> (Refer to the volunteer with the treat.)
>
> "What would happen if my friend here didn't take good care of my things?"
>
> "What if he started stomping on them and destroyed them? (Have the student stomp on the item or tear it apart.)
>
> "What if he opened one up, started licking it, and then decided he didn't like that flavor and just threw it away? (Have the student do this as well.)
>
> "What if he kept losing the suckers I asked him to hold for me? Not a one-time accident, but over and over again, not taking responsibility. Would he be a good helper to me?" (Have the student throw three or four of the items over his shoulder so it's "lost.")

Polka Dot Girls ❀ Self-Control

God has given you and me so many things, and one way we can show Him our appreciation is by taking good care of the stuff He gives us. That means not destroying things. That means not being wasteful with food, or toys, or lots of other stuff. It also means being responsible for the things God has put us in charge of. When we show respect for the things God has given us, it's another way of saying "Thank You!" to God for being so generous with us!

And the last way we can practice self-control with our money is to…

➡ 2. Be Generous.

God gives us money so we can pay our bills, have food to eat, and have clothes to wear. But He also gives us money so we can use it to help other people. We need to always ask Jesus if there's anything special He wants us to do with His money.

There's a story in the Bible about a little boy who was determined to share what he had with Jesus to help other people. Jesus was teaching lots of people—around 4,000 of them! They had been sitting there for a long time, and they were all starting to get really, really hungry! There were no restaurants in those days (So sad—no McDonalds!). Everyone was wondering what to do when a little boy came to Jesus and said, "I will share my lunch!" So Jesus took the boy's lunch, which had five loaves of bread and two fish in it, and prayed over it. Then the coolest miracle happened—God multiplied the food, and there was enough to feed every single person with baskets of food left over!

What I love about this story is that the little boy was willing to share what He had to help others. God has given you lots and lots of things, and He wants you to use those things to help others. So be generous, and always ask Jesus if He wants you to share something you have with someone else. Matthew 10:42 says, *"And if you give even a cup of cold water to one of the least of my followers, you will surely be rewarded."* God might ask you to give someone food, it might be money, it might even be something as simple as a cup of water. But whatever Jesus asks you to do, just do it!

One really important thing to remember when we talk about having self-control with our money is that we need to be really careful how we use the things God has given us.

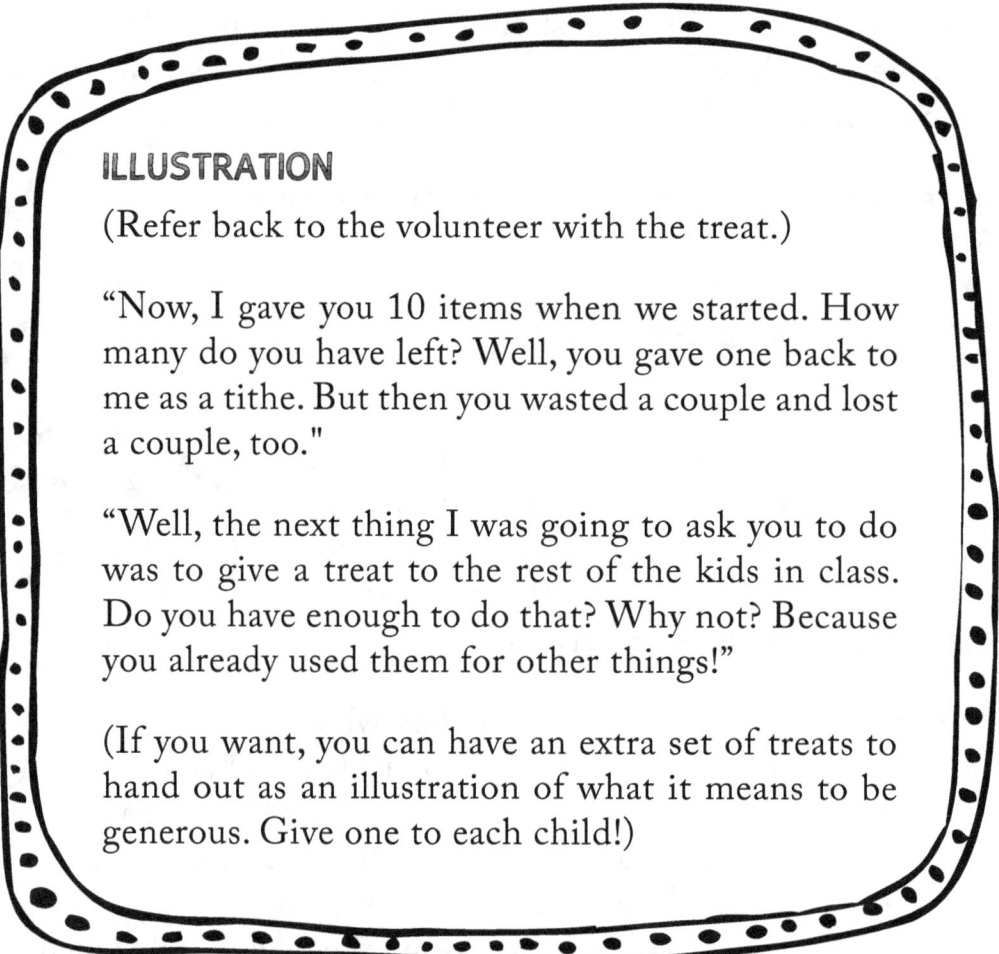

ILLUSTRATION

(Refer back to the volunteer with the treat.)

"Now, I gave you 10 items when we started. How many do you have left? Well, you gave one back to me as a tithe. But then you wasted a couple and lost a couple, too."

"Well, the next thing I was going to ask you to do was to give a treat to the rest of the kids in class. Do you have enough to do that? Why not? Because you already used them for other things!"

(If you want, you can have an extra set of treats to hand out as an illustration of what it means to be generous. Give one to each child!)

It's so fun to have money to spend! As soon as that money finds its way into your pocket, you start imagining all the things you can buy with your cash. Maybe you love to buy gum or candy. Maybe you want to save up for a special toy. Or maybe you want to spend your money on a gift for someone you care about.

But BEFORE you do that, God wants you to STOP, THINK, and ASK Him how He wants you to handle your money. Too often we just go and spend all our money without thinking. Many of us run out and spend our money and then think about it later. But a really good rule to remember is to THINK first, and spend second. Think, "Is this what God wants me to do with my money? Does He want me to be generous to someone first? Should I save this money to buy something bigger later? Are my parents okay with me spending my money this way?"

Don't just spend without thinking! Think first, and then spend!

God wants us to do three things with our money: Share. Save. Spend. Share what you have with God and others. Then save some money for things you may need later. And then spend and enjoy what God has provided for you!

Polka Dot Girls ♣ Self-Control

week 5

Kindergarten and 1st Grade Group Discussion Questions

1. Has anyone ever given you money? What did you buy with your awesome gift?

2. Where does our money **REALLY** come from? Who does our money belong to?

3. One of the biggest ways we can practice self-control with our money is by giving back to God what belongs to Him. Who remembers what a tithe is? Where do we give our tithe, and what does God do with it?

4. Another way we can practice self-control with our money is by taking care of the stuff God gives us. What are some ways we can take care of the things God has given us?

5. What does the word **GENEROUS** mean? How can we be generous?

6. What should we do before we spend money? (*Answer: Stop and think before you spend!*)

7. What three things did we learn that help us take care of the money God gives us? (*Answer: Share. Save. Spend.*)

Polka Dot Girls ❀ Self-Control

week 5

2nd and 3rd Grade Group Discussion Questions

1. Has anyone ever given you money? What did you buy with your awesome gift?

2. Where does our money **REALLY** come from? Who does our money belong to?

3. One of the biggest ways we can practice self-control with our money is by giving back to God what belongs to Him. Who remembers what a tithe is? Where do we give our tithe, and what does God do with it?

4. Another way we can practice self-control with our money is by taking care of the stuff God gives us. What are some ways we can take care of the things God has given us?

5. What does the word **GENEROUS** mean? How can we be generous?

6. What should we do before we spend money? (*Answer: Stop and think before you spend!*)

7. What three things did we learn that help us take care of the money God gives us? (*Answer: Share. Save. Spend.*)

Polka Dot Girls ❀ Self-Control

week 5

4th and 5th Grade Group Discussion Questions

1. Has anyone ever given you money? What did you buy with your awesome gift?

2. Where does our money **REALLY** come from? Who does our money belong to?

3. One of the biggest ways we can practice self-control with our money is by giving back to God what belongs to Him. Who remembers what a tithe is? Where do we give our tithe, and what does God do with it?

4. Another way we can practice self-control with our money is by taking care of the stuff God gives us. What are some ways we can take care of the things God has given us?

5. What does the word **GENEROUS** mean? How can we be generous?

6. What should we do before we spend money? (*Answer: Stop and think before you spend!*)

7. What three things did we learn that help us take care of the money God gives us? (*Answer: Share. Save. Spend.*)

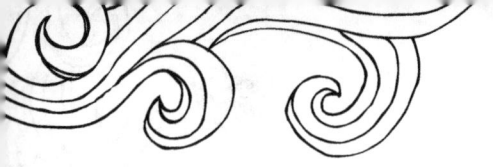

Polka Dot Girls ♣ Self-Control

week 5

Give Back God's Cash

<u>Supplies Needed:</u>
- Standard 15 oz. cans with labels removed or white plastic cups (three per girl)
- Patterned duct tape
- Washi tape
- Standard shipping labels (2"x4")
- Markers
- Template

<u>Prep:</u>
- Copy the cover template onto shipping labels.

<u>What Should We Do Next?</u>
- Give three cans or cups to each girl.
- Older Girls: Wrap each can/cup with their favorite duct and/or washi tape.
- Younger Girls: Depending upon skill, they can wrap their can/cup with duct or washi tape or they can color their cups with markers.
- Give each child three labels—"Share," "Spend," "Save"—to put on their cans/cups.
- When you get money, use the cups to help you decide how you're going to spend what God has given you!

week 5

Parent Partner

Did you know there are more verses in the Bible about money than there are about love? Clearly, God wants us to train up our kids in many areas of life, including handling the resources He gives us! This is one of those areas where your **EXAMPLE** will speak louder than any lesson you could ever teach. It's important to demonstrate with your family resources what it means to live generously. Be consistent in giving, and tell your kids what you're doing. This is a lifelong lesson that will radically affect their lives.

We taught the girls today that everything we have comes from God. He generously gives us resources to use for His purposes. It's important to remember that all our money is God's…we just get to hold onto it for Him!

We shared about tithing and giving God ten percent of all the money we make. I strongly encourage you to start this practice early in your kids' lives. It's an important spiritual discipline that gets harder to implement the older you get!

We also talked about taking good care of the things God gives us. This includes being responsible for our things, not being destructive with our property, and not being wasteful. When we know everything we have belongs to God, there should be a level of respect for the things He has provided for us.

And finally we talked to the girls about generosity. God blesses us so we can bless others. We encouraged the girls to **THINK** before they **SPEND**, asking God if there's some way He would like them to be generous with their money or things. Many times we make impulsive decisions with our money, and then we don't have the resources left to be generous toward others.

God loves to bless His children. Learning the principles of honoring God with our money is important for all of us!

Polka Dot Girls ❦ Self-Control

week 5

Kindergarten and 1st Grade Activity Sheet

John 6:1–15 tells the story of the little boy who shared his lunch with Jesus. Jesus took the fish and bread the boy gave Him and multiplied it to feed thousands of people! On the fish below, draw a picture or write out some things you have that you could share with others.

Our theme verse this week is 2 Corinthians 9:8. In the sentence below, write the word **NEED** in the blank spaces, then practice reading the verse out loud.

"And God will generously provide all you _____. Then you will always have everything you _____ and plenty left over to share with others." (2 Corinthians 9:8)

week 5

2nd and 3rd Grade Activity Sheet

Our theme verse this week is 2 Corinthians 9:8. In the sentence below, write the word **NEED** in two of the blank spaces, and the word **SHARE** in the other blank, then practice reading the verse out loud.

"And God will generously provide all you _____. Then you will always have everything you _____ and plenty left over to _____ with others." (2 Corinthians 9:8)

Use the words about money and generosity below to complete the crossword puzzle.

Across
2. share
6. spend
7. generous
8. resources
9. save
10. money

Down
1. provide
3. responsible
4. belongs
5. tithe
7. give

Polka Dot Girls ❀ Self-Control

week 5

4th and 5th Grade Activity Sheet

Look up 2 Corinthians 9:8 and write it out below. What do you think this verse means?

Use the words about money and generosity below to complete the crossword puzzle.

Across
2. share
6. spend
7. generous
8. resources
9. save
10. money

Down
1. provide
3. responsible
4. belongs
5. tithe
7. give

Polka Dot Girls ❀ Self-Control

Self-Control

week 6

Using My Gifts

What's the Point?

God has given each of us things we're good at, and we need to make sure we're doing everything we can to use our gifts!

theme verse

God has given each of you a gift from his great variety of spiritual gifts. Use them well to serve one another.
1 Peter 4:10

related bible passage

Matthew 25:14–30

❖ Large Group Lesson ❖

Is there something you're REALLY good at doing? Maybe it's playing an instrument or doing science experiments? Maybe you love to read books or bake cakes? Maybe you love to fix things or play soccer?

Every single one of us has things we're good at—EVERY SINGLE ONE OF US. You know how I know that? Because the Bible tells us God has given each of us a gift or a talent. First Peter 4:10 says, "*God has given each of you a gift from his great variety of spiritual gifts. Use them well to serve one another.*" That means when God created you, He made you good at certain things. Your gifts are probably different from my gifts, but you can be sure that God has put gifts inside of YOU!

Wasn't that so nice of God? I think it's pretty cool that He chose to give us things that would bring us so much joy! Our world could have just been filled with boring things that we all felt kind of excited about. Instead, He gave us things that we love, love, love to do!

And because we know our gifts were GIVEN to us by God, we can know God wants us to use our gifts the VERY best way we can. He wants us to work hard and practice and use them as much as possible. So when we talk about having self-control in every area of our lives, we should ask ourselves: Am I being self-controlled in the way I use my gifts?

God gave us talents, and He wants us to USE them. Imagine you pick out a gift for your mom for her birthday. You spend hours thinking about what you're going to get her. Then you spend hours shopping for just the right color and shape. And then you even go above the amount you were planning to spend just because you want to make her day extra special. You give it to her and you're so excited to give her such a special present.

A month later, you see the gift just sitting in the corner, still in the box, gathering dust. I can imagine you'd be pretty frustrated. You might think, "Hey, I spent a lot of time and energy on that gift, and you're doing NOTHING with it." I don't think you'd be very happy.

Some of you aren't taking very good care of the gifts God has given you. They're sitting on a shelf, gathering dust. You're not using the gifts and talents God has placed inside of you. I bet it makes God pretty sad to see gifts He's given us just sitting on the shelf, not being used or taken care of.

There's actually a story in the Bible where Jesus shares how He feels when people neglect the gifts and responsibilities He has given them.

week 6

Illustration: Parable of the Talents

Matthew 25:14–30 (NIRV)

(Have four volunteers come up to the front. One will be the master, and three will be the servants. Have five bags of pennies for the first volunteer, two bags for the second volunteer, and one bag for the third volunteer. Read the story aloud and have the kids act it out.)

"At that time God's kingdom will also be like a man leaving home to travel to another place for a visit. Before he left, he talked with his servants. He told his servants to take care of his things while he was gone. He decided how much each servant would be able to care for. The man gave one servant five bags of money. He gave another servant two bags. And he gave a third servant one bag. Then he left. The servant who got five bags went quickly to invest the money. Those five bags of money earned five more. It was the same with the servant who had two bags. That servant invested the money and earned two more. But the servant who got one bag of money went away and dug a hole in the ground. Then he hid his master's money in the hole.

After a long time the master came home. He asked the servants what they did with his money. The servant who got five bags brought that amount and five more bags of money to the master. The servant said, 'Master, you trusted me to care for five bags of money. So I used them to earn five more.' The master answered, 'You did right. You are a good servant who can be trusted. You did well with that small amount of money. So I will let you care for much greater things. Come and share my happiness with me.' Then the servant who got two bags of money came to the master. The servant said, 'Master, you gave me two bags of money to care for. So I used your two bags to earn two more.' The master answered, 'You did right. You are a good servant who can be trusted. You did well with a small amount of money. So I will let you care for much greater things. Come and share my happiness with me.' Then the servant who got one bag of money came to the master. The servant said, 'Master, I knew you were a very hard man. You harvest what you did not plant. You gather crops where you did not put any seed. So I was afraid. I went and hid your money in the ground. Here is the one bag of money you gave me.' The master answered, 'You are a bad and lazy servant! You say you knew that I harvest what I did not plant and that I gather crops where I did not put any seed. So you should have put my money in the bank. Then, when I came home, I would get my money back. And I would also get the interest that my money earned.' So the master told his other servants, 'Take the one bag of money from that servant and give it to the servant who has ten bags. Everyone who uses what they have will get more. They will have much more than they need. But people who do not use what they have will have everything taken away from them" (Matthew 25:14–30, NIRV).

Yikes! This story is a great example of how God feels when we don't use the gifts He's given us. The master in the story called the servant who didn't use his talents a "bad and lazy servant." I don't know about you, but I don't want to be a "bad and lazy servant"! I want to be a good servant who works hard at my gifts. God gave us gifts to use…so we should use them to the best of our abilities.

How can we have self-control when it comes to our gifts? How can we make sure we're doing the hard work and being a faithful servant with our talents?

⇒ 1. Discover your Gifts.

We've already learned EVERYONE has gifts from God. And we've learned that everyone's gifts are different from everyone else's. The first thing we should do to be faithful with our gifts is to discover what they are!

What are your gifts? What are you good at? What makes you happy? What are some things that come really easy to you? What kind of things do you like learning about? What do you do for fun? At the end of this lesson, we have a quiz that will help you figure it out. Take the quiz, make a list, or ask your friends and family what talents or gifts they see in you. They may have some great ideas!

Kerrigan didn't think she had any gifts. She didn't like to sing or play piano. She didn't like to draw or do ballet like her friends. She always thought gifts were just things you did in music or art class. But one day her mom commented on how God had given her the gift of compassion. She wasn't sure what that meant, so she asked her mom to explain. Her mom said, "Someone with the gift of compassion notices when other people are sad and hurt and wants to help. You always think about other people and go out of your way to make sure they're okay. Not everyone thinks that way, Kerrigan. God made you especially sensitive to other people's feelings so you could reach out and help them. It's a special gift, and it is awesome!"

This was a such a cool moment for Kerrigan! As far back as she could remember, she had a heart for those

who were hurting. It was never something she had to try to do—it was part of who she is.

For some reason, it had never occurred to her that this wasn't an accident. Part of God's design and plan for her life was a soft heart toward people!

This totally changed Kerrigan's life. From that moment on, she paid close attention when her heart was sad for another person. Instead of ignoring the feeling or simply brushing it off, she looked at it as a mission from heaven to reach out to the person God had put in her path.

Maybe your gift is that you care for people like Kerrigan. Maybe you're good at teaching other people. Maybe you're good at playing a certain sport or instrument. Maybe your gift is leading other people, or maybe you love to organize things.

The first way you can make sure you are using self-control with your gifts is to make sure you know what they are. Once you know what you're passionate about, the second thing you need to do is…

➡ 2. Practice, Practice, Practice!

Emily LOVES to play the violin. She started taking lessons when she was little, and she could tell right away that she's good at it. She didn't even have to try very hard when she first started. The music just flew right out of her fingers!

Then her teacher started giving her harder music to play, and she had to spend extra time practicing every day. Pretty soon, she started whining and complaining whenever it was time to practice. Her mom got frustrated, and eventually Emily would get to it, but she didn't have a very good attitude.

Emily's story probably sounds familiar. A lot of us have talents that we're excited to use at first, but having natural talent is only the very beginning of having gifts. We have to practice, learn, and study if we want to grow. That takes a lot of hard work and self-control.

Some of you are really gifted at something, but you've stopped working hard at growing in your gifts. You're not practicing hard. You're not studying. You're

not working hard to get better. The truth is, when it comes to your talent, you'll only get out of it what you put into it. If you're not working at growing your gift, you'll stay at the level you've always been.

But if you practice hard, you'll get better. If you keep working every day, you'll grow stronger. You'll be like the servant in the story who pleased the Master because he worked hard to make sure he used what he'd been given and multiplied it into something more.

Ecclesiastes 9:10 says, "*Whatever you are capable of doing, do with all your might…*" That means you work your hardest. You practice every day. You go to classes and lessons and ask questions so you can get better.

So, we need to discover our gifts, practice hard, and lastly…

➡ 3. SHARE our Gifts with Others!

I think there are a lot of people in the world who **KNOW** what their gifts are, but they're too scared to **SHARE** their gifts with others. Maybe they love to sing but would **NEVER** sing in front of other people. Maybe they **LOVE** to play basketball in the yard with their family, but they're too nervous to join a team and play when other people are watching. Maybe they love to build things, but they never show anyone what they've made because they're scared of what other people might think.

God gave you gifts because He wants you to use them to help others! Look at our theme verse again: "*God has given each of you a gift from his great variety of spiritual gifts. Use them well to serve one another*" (1 Peter 4:10). What does that second part say? **USE THEM WELL TO SERVE ONE ANOTHER!**

If you're not sharing your gifts with others, you're missing out on one of the great joys of life!

Many times we're just scared to use our gifts. We don't want to look silly, or we're afraid we won't do a good job. Remember the third servant in the our story in Matthew? He hid his gift! He said, "I was afraid." He was afraid of other people's reactions. He was afraid of failing. He was unsure of his own abilities. He just stopped trying.

week 6

Maybe someone has said something mean to you or made fun of you when you've tried to use your gift in the past. Sometimes it can be hard to get past a bad experience. Maybe someone has mistreated your gift.

I know this can be so hard, but don't fall for it! Don't allow someone else to keep you from what God has for you. Even if it's scary, remind yourself that God has plans for you and your talents.

When I've faced this situation, it's helped me to refocus my attention away from what OTHER people think of me and determine that it is far more important for me to please my Heavenly Father than any other person. I remember Galatians 1:10: "*If I were still trying to please men, I would not be Christ's servant.*" Do not allow another person to convince you that your gift has no value. Do not let your fear of what other people might say keep you sidelined. Decide to use your talents as a faithful servant of Jesus, and let Him deal with the people who would try to discourage you.

If your gift is sitting on a shelf gathering dust, it's time to take it down and start using it again!

First Timothy 4:14–16 says, "*…that special gift of ministry you were given when the leaders of the church laid hands on you and prayed—keep that dusted off and in use. Cultivate these things. Immerse yourself in them. The people will all see you mature right before their eyes! Keep a firm grasp on both your character and your teaching. Don't be diverted. Just keep at it*" (MSG).

God has given you gifts. Discover what they are. Faithfully practice and grow them. Faithfully share them with others.

Polka Dot Girls ♣ Self-Control

week 6

Kindergarten and 1st Grade Group Discussion Questions

1. Where do our gifts come from? Does everyone have one?

2. Let's practice saying this week's theme verse: "*God has given each of you a gift from his great variety of spiritual **gifts**. Use them well to serve one another.*" (1 Peter 4:10)

3. Share one thing you're good at. Maybe it's a talent, a sport, a hobby, something at school, or even something about your personality that's unique and brings you or others joy.

4. What are some ways we can grow in our gifts? (*Possible Answers: Practice every day. Study—learn more. Ask people who are good at your talent to show you how to get better. Keep looking for opportunities to learn more about your talents.*)

5. Why do you think it's so easy to put our gifts up on a shelf? Think of an area where you've allowed fear or a bad experience to cause you to give up on a gift or talent?

6. Take a minute to brainstorm some creative new ways to use your gifts.

Polka Dot Girls ❀ Self-Control

week 6

2nd and 3rd Grade Group Discussion Questions

1. Where do our gifts come from? Does everyone have one?

2. Let's practice saying this week's theme verse: "*God has given each of you a gift from his great variety of spiritual **gifts**. Use them well to serve one another.*" (1 Peter 4:10)

3. Share one thing you're good at. Maybe it's a talent, a sport, a hobby, something at school, or even something about your personality that's unique and brings you or others joy.

4. What are some ways we can grow in our gifts? (*Possible Answers: Practice every day. Study—learn more. Ask people who are good at your talent to show you how to get better. Keep looking for opportunities to learn more about your talents.*)

5. Why do you think it's so easy to put our gifts up on a shelf? Think of an area where you've allowed fear or a bad experience to cause you to give up on a gift or talent?

6. When other people cheer us on, it's easier to use our gifts. What are some ways you can encourage your friends and family to use their gifts?

7. Take a minute to brainstorm some creative new ways to use your gifts.

Polka Dot Girls ❀ Self-Control

week 6

4th and 5th Grade Group Discussion Questions

1. Where do our gifts come from? Does everyone have one?

2. Let's practice saying this week's theme verse: "*God has given each of you a gift from his great variety of spiritual **gifts**. Use them well to serve one another.*" (1 Peter 4:10)

3. Share one thing you're good at. Maybe it's a talent, a sport, a hobby, something at school, or even something about your personality that's unique and brings you or others joy.

4. What are some ways we can grow in our gifts? (*Possible Answers: Practice every day. Study—learn more. Ask people who are good at your talent to show you how to get better. Keep looking for opportunities to learn more about your talents.*)

5. Who are some people who could help you grow in your gifts?

6. Why do you think it's so easy to put our gifts up on a shelf? Think of an area where you've allowed fear or a bad experience to cause you to give up on a gift or talent?

7. When other people cheer us on, it's easier to use our gifts. What are some ways you can encourage your friends and family to use their gifts?

8. Take a minute to brainstorm some creative new ways to use your gifts.

Polka Dot Girls ❀ Self-Control

week 6

Practice My Gifts!

<u>Supplies Needed:</u>
- Cardstock
- Crayons and/or Markers
- Pretty Embellishments
- Template

<u>Prep:</u>
- Copy the template onto the white cardstock.

<u>What Should We Do Next?</u>
- Color the practice sheet.

Tell each girl to hang this practice sheet on their fridge or in their room. They should color a circle every time they practice their gift. Remind them that God has given each of them a gift and it's important to practice so they can share their gifts with others and glorify God.

God has given each of you a gift from his great variety of spiritual gifts.
Use them well to serve one another.
−1 Peter 4:10

Month: _____

week 6

Parent Partner

One of the most enjoyable things about parenting is discovering your kids' unique gifts and talents. There's nothing more fun than watching them unearth their passions and seeing them excel in their own unique ways.

One of the most challenging things in parenting is learning how to help your child embrace their own gifts without comparing themselves to others. Sometimes our kids may not even realize the ways God has uniquely designed them to impact the world. Keep your eyes open for areas of passion and interest in your child and do everything you can to encourage them in these areas.

Having self-control when it comes to your gifts is a very important aspect of growth. There are many talented people who never measure up to their full potential because they lack the discipline to develop their natural abilities through hard work and practice. This week, we encouraged the girls to work diligently at their gifts and talents. Even when it's hard, we need to recognize that God has given us gifts for a purpose. It's our responsibility to use them to the best of our ability.

It's not enough to just know what our talents are—God wants us to USE them! There are so many gifted people in the world who aren't using the gifts God has given them. Encourage your daughter to overcome fear and worry of what others will think and bravely use her talents.

We reminded the girls of Philippians 4:13: *"I can do everything through Christ, who gives me strength."* Remind your daughter that, even if she's scared, God will help her do her very best!

Polka Dot Girls ♣ Self-Control

week 6

Kindergarten and 1st Grade Take Home Activity Sheet

Our theme verse is 1 Peter 4:10. In the blank, fill in the word GIFTS!

"God has given each of you a gift from his great variety of spiritual _____. Use them well to serve one another." –1 Peter 4:10

Fill in the blanks to help discover your gifts and talents.

If I have an afternoon to myself, I love to _____.

My favorite subject in school is _____.

If I could volunteer to help somewhere, I would choose to help with _____ _____.

I love to _____.

I want to learn more about _____.

My favorite hobbies are _____.

I'm happiest when I'm _____.

People say that I'm _____.

I feel really proud when I'm _____.

Draw a picture of you doing your favorite thing.

Polka Dot Girls ❈ Self-Control

week 6

2nd and 3rd Grade
Take Home Activity Sheet

Look up 1 Peter 4:10 in your Bible and write it in the space provided.

Fill in the blanks to help discover your gifts and talents.

If I have an afternoon to myself, I love to _____.

My favorite subject in school is _____.

If I could volunteer to help somewhere, I would choose to help with _____.

I love to _____.

I want to learn more about _____.

My favorite hobbies are _____.

I'm happiest when I'm _____.

People say that I'm _____.

I feel really proud when I'm _____.

Polka Dot Girls ❀ Self-Control

week 6

Here's a list of some gifts and talents. Circle anything you're good at.

Being kind

Caring about other people

Movies
(reviewing, writing, filming, story, acting)

Photography

Author
(writing stories or articles)

Technology
(setting up blogs, fixing computers)

Thinking
(arguing, debating, worldview, philosophy)

Politics & government

Being responsible

Friendship

Helping your family or teachers

Taking care of God's creation

Telling others about Jesus

Starting new things

Memorizing things

Music

Sports

School

Science

Reading

Inventing

Listening to other people's problems

Visiting people who are sick or sad

Doing thoughtful things for others

Building things

Smiling

Going on adventures

Acting or drama

Art
(drawing, painting, making)

Board games, strategy games

Building, construction, carpentry

Organizing things

Solving puzzles & mysteries

Leading a group

Giving things to others

Sharing

Praying for others

Studying the Bible

Teaching

Cooking

Crafts

Electronics
(computers, coding, video games)

Fashion design, sewing

Gardening
(veggies, herbs, flowers)

Graphics Arts
(typography, Illustrator, Photoshop)

House renovations & maintenance

Interior decorating

Mechanics
(small motors, fixing things)

Of the things you circled, write your three FAVORITES below:

1. _____

2. _____

3. _____

week 6

4th and 5th Grade Take Home Activity Sheet

Look up 1 Peter 4:10 in your Bible and write it in the space provided.

Fill in the blanks to help discover your gifts and talents.

If I have an afternoon to myself, I love to _____.

My favorite subject in school is _____.

If I could volunteer to help somewhere, I would choose to help with _____.

I love to _____.

I want to learn more about _____.

My favorite hobbies are _____.

I'm happiest when I'm _____.

People say that I'm _____.

I feel really proud when I'm _____.

Polka Dot Girls ❀ Self-Control

week 6

Here's a list of some gifts and talents. Circle anything you're good at.

Being kind

Caring about other people

Movies
(reviewing, writing, filming, story, acting)

Photography

Author
(writing stories or articles)

Technology
(setting up blogs, fixing computers)

Thinking
(arguing, debating, worldview, philosophy)

Politics & government

Being responsible

Friendship

Helping your family or teachers

Taking care of God's creation

Telling others about Jesus

Starting new things

Memorizing things

Music

Sports

School

Science

Reading

Inventing

Listening to other people's problems

Visiting people who are sick or sad

Doing thoughtful things for others

Building things

Smiling

Going on adventures

Acting or drama

Art
(drawing, painting, making)

Board games, strategy games

Building, construction, carpentry

Organizing things

Solving puzzles & mysteries

Leading a group

Giving things to others

Sharing

Praying for others

Studying the Bible

Teaching

Cooking

Crafts

Electronics
(computers, coding, video games)

Fashion design, sewing

Gardening
(veggies, herbs, flowers)

Graphics Arts
(typography, Illustrator, Photoshop)

House renovations & maintenance

Interior decorating

Mechanics
(small motors, fixing things)

Of the things you circled, write your three FAVORITES below:

1. _____

2. _____

3. _____

In the space provided, write out three things you can do to get better at your gifts.

What are three ways you could start using your gifts RIGHT NOW?

Polka Dot Girls ❖ Self-Control

Self-Control

week 7

Taking My Time

What's the Point?

God wants us to be smart about how we use our time.

theme verse

There is a right time for everything...
Ecclesiastes 3:1 (ERV)

related bible passage
Daniel 1: 17–21

❋ Large Group Lesson ❋

Do you know how many hours are in a day? 24.

Do you know how many minutes are in a day? 1,440.

Do you know how many seconds are in a day? 86,400.

When God made the world, He started TIME. He caused the sun to rise in the morning and set in the evening, created morning and night, and gave us days and weeks and years. TIME is something God created.

He gives each and every one of us the same amount of hours, minutes, and seconds in a day. No one gets more. No one gets less. You can't buy more hours for your day.

God wants us to be smart about how we use the time He has given us. Psalm 90:12 says, "*Teach us to number our days, that we may gain a heart of wisdom.*" God wants us to realize that every day is precious and we need to make good use of the time He has given us.

God has a plan for every single day of your life. Not one day is wasted. There's not one day that's unimportant. Psalm 139:16 says, "*Every day of my life was recorded in Your book. Every moment was laid out before a single day had passed.*" Every day is important and filled with things God has planned for you to do!

So why is it so easy to manage our time poorly? Why do we sometimes waste too much time on things that aren't important? Why do we sometimes waste time doing the things we know we shouldn't be doing?

Kallie was having a hard time managing her time. Most of her days looked like this: Her Mom would wake her up for school, but she would have a hard time getting up. (She had stayed up extra late the night before watching TV, so she was just *so* tired!) She would lie in bed until she was late and her Mom would yell at her from the kitchen. She would race out of bed, grab some dirty, wrinkly clothes, and race down to breakfast. After she ate, she would run to put her lunch in her backpack and realize she had forgotten to do yesterday's homework assignment! She had meant to do it, but when she got home, she got distracted by her iPad and never got back to it. Oops.

As Kallie raced onto the bus, she wasn't feeling very good about herself. Why was she always forgetting things? Why was she always late? Why couldn't she get her act together?

The truth is, that Kallie was not practicing self-control when it came to her time. She wasn't making good choices about how she spent her minutes. She just went with whatever she felt like doing in the moment instead of making decisions based on what was the best use of her time. She needed to make a plan to manage her time better and then stick to it!

God wants us to be wise with the time He has given us every day.

week 7

Here are three places we need to have self-control with our time.

➡ 1. Have Self-Control in your Work Time.

Do you have a job? I'm guessing that none of you get up in the morning, put on a suit and grab a briefcase, and head out to work! But you DO have work that you are responsible for every single day—going to school and doing your very best with your studies, chores and responsibilities at home, things you're committed to (sports teams, music lessons, other clubs or classes).

The first and most important area where you learn to manage your time well is your work. God wants you to be a hard worker. Colossians 3:23 says, "*In all the work you are given, do the best you can. Work as though you are working for the Lord, not any earthly master*" (ERV).

God wants you to work hard! He wants you to do your very best. He wants you to be dependable and responsible. There are lots of reasons this is important, but do you know one of the most important reasons you should be self-controlled with your time? It's is a great way to show others you love Jesus!

There's a story in the Bible about a boy named Daniel and his friends, who were captured and taken to Babylon to be put in the king's service. Everyone watched to see how these four young men would handle this tough situation. This is what the Bible says about Daniel and his friends:

"*Every time the king asked them about something important, they showed great wisdom and understanding. The king found they were ten times better than all the magicians and wise men in his kingdom*" (Daniel 1:20, ERV).

The King and all the other people in the kingdom took note that Daniel and his friends were smart, helpful, and worked hard. It didn't matter what kind of situation they were in, they determined to do their very best no matter what.

My prayer is that any teacher, coach, or friend you have contact with finds you ten times better than anyone else around—just like Daniel! When they ask you why, you'll be able to share that you work hard because you love God and the Bible tells you to!

A lot of people WANT to be ten times better at stuff, but they're not willing to do the hard work to get there. Proverbs 13:4 says, *"Lazy people always want things but never get them. Those who work hard get plenty."* (ERV). So make sure you're studying hard. Make sure you're practicing what you're supposed to be practicing. Make sure you show up on time and don't skip out on things you've committed to.

Determine to be a hard worker today! Show up on time. Get your homework done. Make sure you do your chores well, and without complaining. Be a good manager of your time.

➡ 2. Have Self-Control in your Play Time.

Bethany was so excited for Saturday, she could hardly wait! She had a long week at school with so much homework that she couldn't wait to have a day off. She started watching a marathon of one of her favorite shows on her computer, and she just kept watching and watching and watching. After a while, she started feeling kind of yucky. Her muscles were feeling sore and she was feeling super blah. Her mom came upstairs and asked her how long she had been watching her show, and Bethany realized it had been four hours! Her mom was not very happy with her, and she was not very happy with herself, either.

How many of you have limits on your computer or iPad time? How many of you have rules about how much TV you can watch? How many of you have rules about how many video games you can play? Why do you think your parents give you rules like that?

It's not good for us to spend too much time doing those things. It's super fun to be able to play fun games and watch good movies or TV shows, but many of us have a hard time practicing self-control. Sometimes we do it as LONG as we can get away with (before our parents realize what we've been doing),

week 7

but I want to challenge you—YOU are supposed to be the one who shows self-control with your time. YOU are in charge of the minutes God has given you. Instead of just trying to get away with as much as you can get away with, think about what a healthy time limit is and talk about it with your parents. Then YOU take responsibility for staying within those time limits. Maybe you need to set a timer for yourself. Maybe you need to commit to watching one episode of something at a time instead of watching 25!

One of the BIGGEST ways you can practice self-control is by making good choices in how you handle your play time!

And the last way you can practice self-control with your time is to…

⇨ 3. Have Self-Control in your Rest Time.

Have you ever thought about how weird it is that we all SLEEP every night? It gets dark outside, we all go into our rooms and crawl into bed, and we pretty much don't know what's going on around us for eight or nine hours. It's weird!

But God designed our bodies to need sleep and God designed our bodies to need rest! If our bodies and minds don't have time to just check out and recover, pretty soon they start wearing down and getting sick.
So we need to practice self-control in how we rest!

That means you need to make sure you're getting enough sleep! Remember our story about Kallie, who had such a hard time getting out of bed? Part of her problem was that she wasn't making good choices about getting enough sleep so she could work hard the next day. She was simply doing what she wanted to do at the moment without thinking about how it would affect her ability to do her best at school the next day. (Hmm…Do you remember learning about "I want what I want when I want it"? Seems like Kallie needs to push down the flesh and have self-

control!) God wants you to do your best every day. That starts with doing your best to get a good night's sleep.

Another really important way God wants us to rest is by observing a SABBATH. Do you know what a Sabbath is? It's kind of a funny word! A Sabbath is a day set aside to rest. The word Sabbath actually means "to stop"! We first read about it in Exodus 20:8–10: *"You must remember to keep the Sabbath a special day. You may work six days a week to do your job. But the seventh day is a day of rest in honor of the Lord your God"* (ERV).

This is actually one of the Ten Commandments! (Which, surprisingly, most of us don't do a very good job at keeping! I'm glad we don't take this same approach with "thou shall not kill!")

Basically, a Sabbath is a day when we take the time to rest and worship. We step away from our normal routine and allow ourselves time to reflect, connect with our families, and rest our bodies.

The Bible is very clear that you and I should set aside time every single week for REST. Now, resting might mean taking a nice long nap for some of us, but resting can mean a whole lot of other things, too. You can rest by going for a nice walk with your family. You can rest by cooking a meal or playing a game. You can rest by reading a book or throwing around a baseball. Resting means doing something you enjoy in a relaxed environment. Think about what makes you feel refreshed and ready to take on another day. Whatever those things are, you should make sure you take the time to do those things once a week.

Polka Dot Girls ❁ Self-Control

week 6

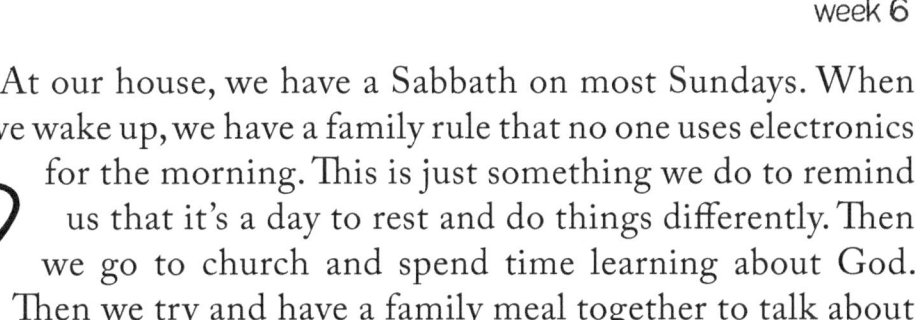

At our house, we have a Sabbath on most Sundays. When we wake up, we have a family rule that no one uses electronics for the morning. This is just something we do to remind us that it's a day to rest and do things differently. Then we go to church and spend time learning about God. Then we try and have a family meal together to talk about the next week and all that's coming up. Then we each do some things that we personally enjoy.

Everybody's Sabbath may look different. Your family may have a Saturday night Sabbath where you have family time and rest. Maybe you have some quiet time during another part of the week. Talk to your parents about ways you can plan some rest time into your family routine every week. God wants to take good care of us, and He tells us over and over in the Bible that we should make sure we have self-control when it comes to having times of rest!

God wants you to have discipline when it comes to your time. Whether you're at work, at play, or at rest, do your very best with the time God has given you every single day!

Polka Dot Girls ✤ Self-Control

week 7

Kindergarten and 1st Grade Group Discussion Questions

1. How many hours are there in a day? Does anyone get more or less than that?

2. Why is it so important to be careful about how we use our time? (*Answer: Because God has a plan for each of our days, and if we don't use our time well, we'll miss it!*)

3. What is your WORK? In other words, what are the responsibilities you have every day? (*Possible Answers: school, chores, practice, lessons*)

4. What are some ways you can have more self-control in your work?

5. Is it hard to practice self-control when it comes to your play time? Why do you think that is?

6. What are some ways you can make sure you rest every week?

Polka Dot Girls ✿ Self-Control

week 7

2nd and 3rd Grade Group Discussion Questions

1. How many hours are there in a day? Does anyone get more or less than that?

2. Why is it so important to be careful about how we use our time? (*Answer: Because God has a plan for each of our days, and if we don't use our time well, we'll miss it!*)

3. What is your WORK? In other words, what are the responsibilities you have every day? (*Possible Answers: school, chores, practice, lessons*)

4. What are some ways you can have more self-control in your work?

5. Is it hard to practice self-control when it comes to your play time? Why do you think that is?

6. What can you do to be better about limits during your play time?

7. What's a Sabbath?

8. What are some ways you can make sure you rest every week?

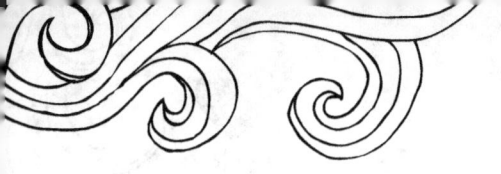

Polka Dot Girls ❖ Self-Control

week 7

4th and 5th Grade Group Discussion Questions

1. How many hours are there in a day? Does anyone get more or less than that?

2. Why is it so important to be careful about how we use our time? (*Answer: Because God has a plan for each of our days, and if we don't use our time well, we'll miss it!*)

3. What is your WORK? In other words, what are the responsibilities you have every day? (*Possible Answers: school, chores, practice, lessons*)

4. What are some ways you can have more self-control in your work?

5. Is it hard to practice self-control when it comes to your play time? Why do you think that is?

6. Often we try to get away with as much as we can instead of taking responsibility to set limits for ourselves. Why do you think we do this?

7. What can you do to be better about limits during your play time?

8. What's a Sabbath?

9. Sometimes the things we THINK are relaxing (like using electronics or watching TV) aren't truly giving us rest. What other things can you do to rest?

10. Share one thing you're going to do to practice a Sabbath this week.

Polka Dot Girls ❀ Self-Control

week 7

Taking My Time Door Hanger

<u>Supplies Needed:</u>
- Foam Door Hanger
- Permanent Markers (variety of colors)
- Wooden Clothes Pins (5 or 6 per girl)
- Foam Stickers (optional)

<u>Prep:</u>
- For younger children, use a permanent marker to write "TO DO" on the left side under the opening and write DONE on the right side.
- For younger children, use a permanent marker to write different types of chores on the wooden close pins (brush teeth, make bed, take out garbage, load dishes, unload dishes, read, etc.)

<u>What Should We Do Next?</u>
- Use a permanent marker to write on the foam door hanger:
  - Write "TO DO" on the left side under the opening.
  - Write "DONE" on the right side under the opening.
- Use a permanent marker to write different types of chores on each clothes pin (brush teeth, make bed, take out garbage, load dishes, unload dishes, read, etc.).
- Decorate the door hanger with foam stickers (optional).
- Have the girls put the doorhanger in a place they will see it every day. Once they've completed their chores, move the clothes pin from the "To Do" side to the "Done" side.

Parent Partner

Most days I struggle to manage my time well. I'm guessing some of you do, too. Kids are no different. As we look at practicing self-control in every area of our lives, this is certainly an area where we need all the help we can get!

Colossians 3:23 says, *"In all the work you are given, do the best you can. Work as though you are working for the Lord, not an earthly master"* (ERV). We encouraged the girls to practice discipline when it comes to their work time—school, homework, chores, extra curricular activities. They learned that making wise choices with their time and work ethic will help them stand out from the crowd and show people they love Jesus.

Second, we challenged the kids to practice self-control in their play time. We all know the battle of getting our kids to regulate their screen time! We challenged the girls to take responsibility for a balanced approach to play time rather than trying to get away with as much as they can.

Last, we taught the girls about getting adequate rest and honoring a Sabbath. Many of our kids have no idea how to actually rest and allow their bodies and minds to be replenished. You can set the example for your kids by showing them what a balanced life looks like. Make sure you're intentional about seasons of rest for your family. It's a lifelong lesson they will thank you for someday!

week 7

Kindergarten and 1st Grade Take Home Activity Sheet

On the clock below, draw a picture or write a list of some things you do for your work time, play time, and rest time every day.

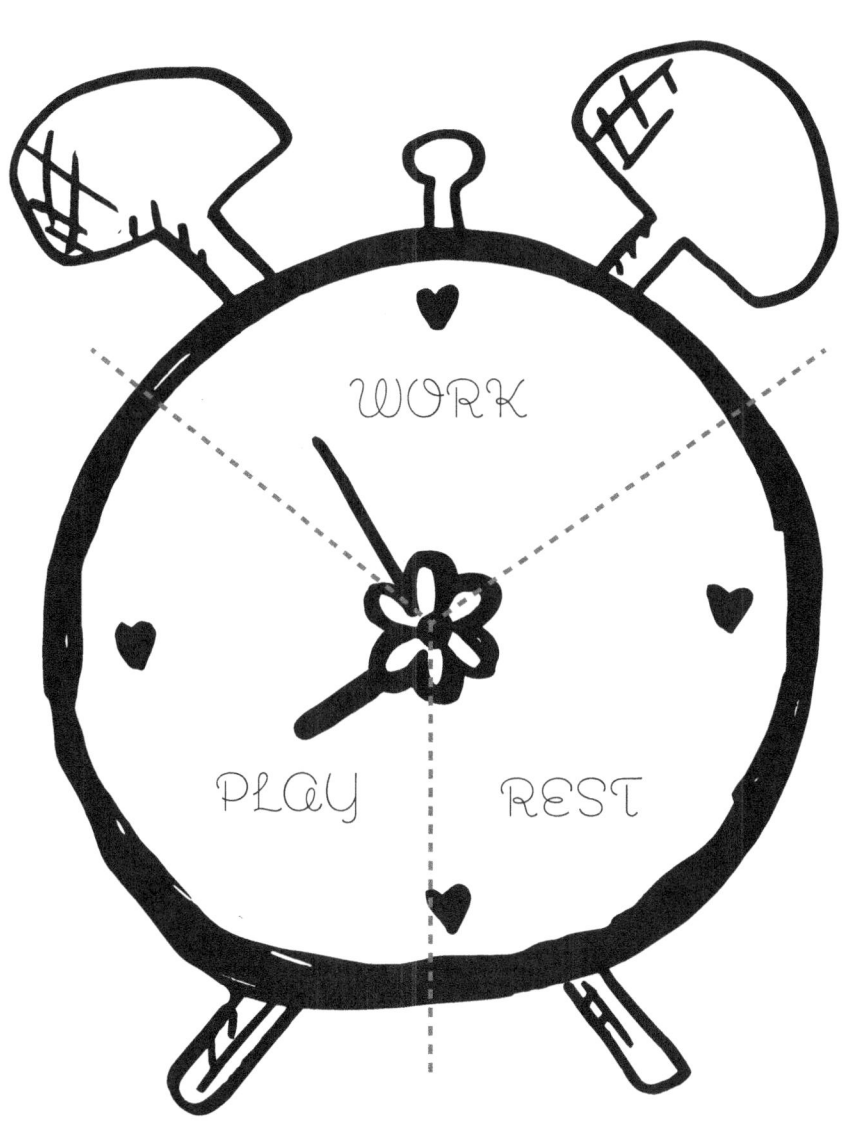

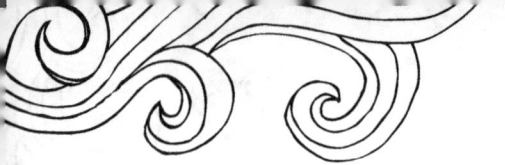

Find the words in the puzzle!

```
Q K P X S U R K F
H C G L L R I G Y
P O T L A Z U Z O
S L L U T Y I O A
A C H W O R K F H
D N N E V V F I Z
X U M L D G P W V
P I M R J J I A U
T S O N B D Z M M
```

Word List

Clock

Hours

Play

Time

Work

Polka Dot Girls ❀ Self-Control

week 7

2nd and 3rd Grade
Take Home Activity Sheet

On the clock below, draw a picture or write a list of some things you do for your work time, play time, and rest time every day.

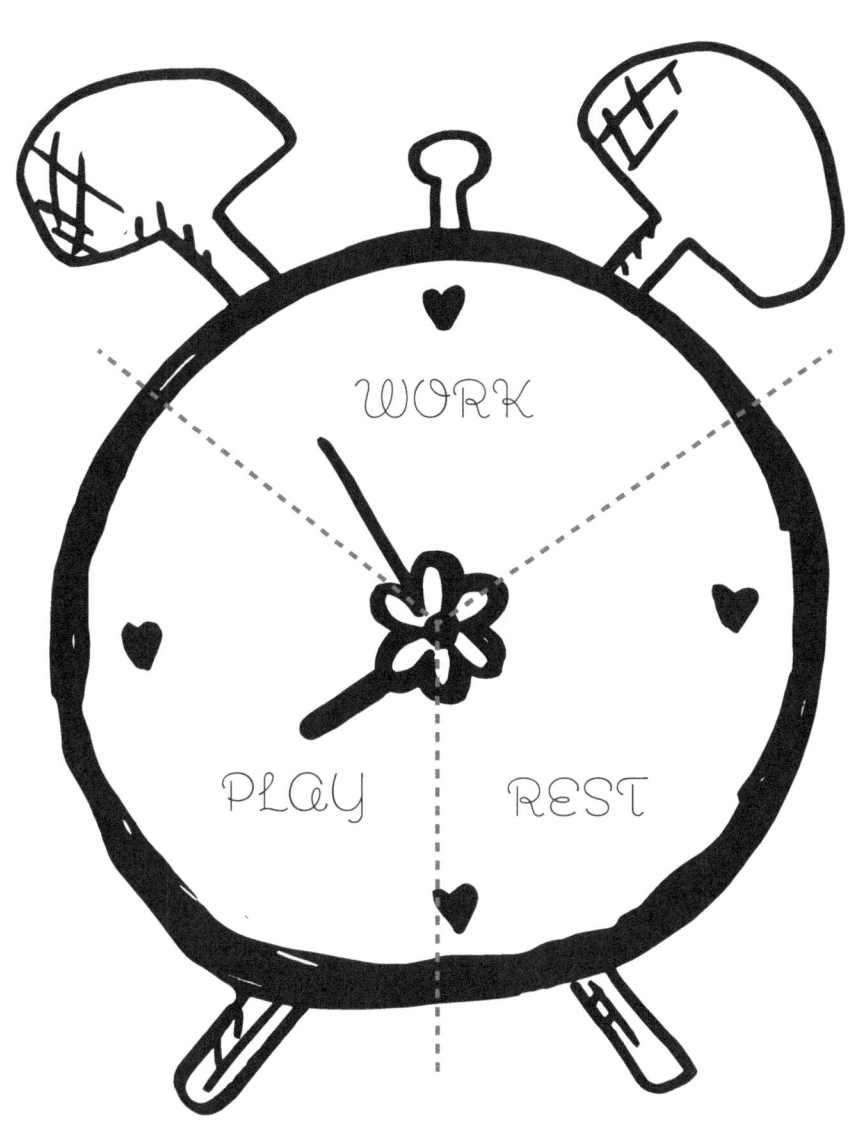

Use the word list below to fill in the blanks and complete these verses.

Psalm 139:16

Every _____ of my life was recorded in Your book.

Every _____ was laid out before a single had passed.

Ecclesiastes 3:1

There is a right _____ for everything.

Psalm 90:12

Teach us to number our days that we may gain a heart of _____.

Colossians 3:23

In all the _____ you are given, do the best you can. Work as though you are working for the Lord, not any earthly master.

Proverbs 13:4

_____ people always want things but never get them. Those who work hard get plenty.

Exodus 20:8

You must remember to keep the _____ as a special day.

Word List:

Sabbath

Time

Day

Lazy

Wisdom

Work

Day

Polka Dot Girls ❀ Self-Control

week 7

Find the words in the puzzle below!

```
V S M Z P Y E C T T H C Y V S
M R P T I M Z K X H H K A P Z
R T D Q X T P A E U T A D D Z
H O U R S N O R L X A H Y U F
T O F H J I G J C R B T K K N
Z P L U H S M Z E W B P B U Q
S R I G S M W C X T A Y A L P
P O V J Z Y B V N V S L V H N
R R I U W J U Z N P P I V H M
C D E Y A O B Y F Y Q M Y O V
W L G W P H T O H J S G D R F
I A O P Z T I Y L S T S N J M
J R K C U A M F N R I D D G I
K X X Z K F E J L W V L L B T
V C Z R A P I E A I D C V P N
```

Word List:

Clock

Day

Hours

Lazy

Play

Sabbath

Time

Wisdom

Work

Polka Dot Girls ❀ Self-Control

week 7

4th and 5th Grade Take Home Activity Sheet

Use the word list below to fill in the blanks and complete these verses.

Psalm 139:16

Every _____ of my life was recorded in Your book.

Every _____ was laid out before a single had passed.

Ecclesiastes 3:1

There is a right _____ for everything.

Psalm 90:12

Teach us to number our days that we may gain a heart of _____.

Colossians 3:23

In all the _____ you are given, do the best you can. Work as though you are working for the Lord, not any earthly master.

Proverbs 13:4

_____ people always want things but never get them. Those who work hard get plenty.

Exodus 20:8

You must remember to keep the _____ as a special day.

Word List:

Sabbath Lazy Day

Time Wisdom

Day Work

Find the words in the puzzle below!

```
V S M Z P Y E C T T H C Y V S
M R P T I M Z K X H H K A P Z
R T D Q X T P A E U T A D D Z
H O U R S N O R L X A H Y U F
T O F H J I G J C R B T K K N
Z P L U H S M Z E W B P B U Q
S R I G S M W C X T A Y A L P
P O V J Z Y B V N V S L V H N
R R I U W J U Z N P P I V H M
C D E Y A O B Y F Y Q M Y O V
W L G W P H T O H J S G D R F
I A O P Z T I Y L S T S N J M
J R K C U A M F N R I D D G I
K X X Z K F E J L W V L L B T
V C Z R A P I E A I D C V P N
```

Word List:

Clock

Day

Hours

Lazy

Play

Sabbath

Time

Wisdom

Work

Polka Dot Girls ❧ Self-Control

week 7

Read the story of Daniel in Daniel 1. In the blanks below, write three things Daniel did that set him apart from all the other people.

1. _____

2. _____

3. _____

What can you learn from Daniel's example?

Polka Dot Girls ❀ Self-Control

The Way to Obey

What's the Point?

God wants us to obey, without delay, all the way, the right way!

theme verse

Children, obey your parents the way the Lord wants, because this is the right thing to do.

Ephesians 6:1 (ERV)

related bible passage

Numbers 20:1–13

❀ Large Group Lesson ❀

Have you ever played "Simon Says?" You know, the game where the leader tells you what to do and you have to do whatever they say? It's such a fun game to play, especially if you get to be the one telling everyone what to do. OH, THE POWER! Mwahhhhhhhhaaaa! (Insert evil laugh here.) It's fun to be in charge of other people!

It's super fun to be the leader in "Simon Says," and it's still kind of fun to be the one following directions. But it isn't always fun to have to do what other people tell you to do in real life. Like when your mom tells you to do your homework before playing with your friends (ugh!). Or when your teacher tells you to stop talking to your neighbor and finish your assignment (double ugh!). Or when

your dad tells you to organize the garage while your friends are all going to the movies (triple super-duper ugh!).

God puts people in our lives who are kind of the boss of us while we're young. Romans 13:1 says, *"For all authority comes from God, and those in positions of authority have been placed there by God"*. These people have been put in authority by God to take care of us and help us grow. They keep us safe and teach us how to become good, responsible people. These people are your parents, teachers, leaders, pastors, coaches, and others in positions of authority over you. God wants us to honor them in many ways, including speaking respectfully, listening to what they say, and most importantly, obeying them.

OBEY—that's kind of a funny word, isn't it? Do you know what it means? It means to do whatever someone in authority over you tells you to do. It means to follow their instructions or commands. It means listening to directions and following those directions.

It's very important to remember that, first and foremost, God wants us to obey Him. He has given us instructions in the Bible, and it matters a lot to Him that we obey those instructions. Jeremiah 42:6 says, *"Whether we like it or not, we will obey the Lord our God to whom we are sending you with our plea. For if we obey him, everything will turn out well for us"*. Sometimes we may not want to do the right thing, but this verse reminds us that when we choose to do the things God has told us to do (and when we choose NOT to do the things God has told us NOT to do), things will go well for us. If we choose to disobey God, we're going to have some problems and things will not go well for us. But if we follow His instructions, He has promised to lead us on the best possible path for our lives!

God wants us to obey Him, and He wants us to obey the authority figures He has put in our lives. Ephesians 6:1 tells us, *"Children, obey your parents the way the Lord wants, because this is the right thing to do"* (ERV). Obeying your parents, teachers, and leaders is an important part of growing up and honoring God with your life.

That's not always easy, is it?

Polka Dot Girls ✤ Self-Control

week 8

Sometimes we just don't feel like doing what we've been told to do. Sometimes we don't like the instructions we've been given. Sometimes we're just lazy or want to do things our own way. Obedience might seem like a simple idea, but it's certainly not easy!

If we want to honor God, we need to learn to obey. So here are three ways we can honor God with our obedience.

The first way, is to…

➡ 1. Obey without Delay!

When Annabeth got home from school one day, she was exhausted. She dropped her coat and backpack on the floor in the hallway and ran to the kitchen to grab a granola bar and juice box. Her mom yelled down the stairs, "Annabeth! Make sure you hang up your coat and backpack!"

Annabeth yelled back, "Okay," but she was digging through the box for her favorite flavor of juice box and was distracted by all the yumminess. Once she found just the right beverage, she remembered she wanted to check her iPad to see if there was a message from her friend about meeting at the park, so she ran to the desk when she heard her mom yell down the stairs again, "Annabeth, did you hang up your coat and backpack?" She yelled back, "Just a minute!" as she scrolled through her messages looking for a reply. She really intended to go hang up her backpack just as soon as she replied to her friend, but she remembered that she was in the middle of a super awesome game and was JUST about to finish a level, so she sat down and started playing.

A few minutes later, she looked up to see her mom standing in front of her with a not-so-happy look on her face. "Annabeth! I told you to pick up your coat and backpack!" Annabeth, suddenly remembered what she was supposed to do and felt bad that she hadn't obeyed her mother right away. She meant to do it, but she got distracted and ended up disobeying what her mother had said to do.

When our parents, teachers, or coaches ask us to do something, we need to obey RIGHT THEN. It's not okay to say, "I'll eventually get to it," or "I'll do it later!" That is not obeying. It's also not

183

okay to ignore someone when they're giving you instructions or put off doing the thing they tell you to do. Being obedient means immediately doing the thing being asked of us, not waiting until later, not getting around to it eventually, not ignoring instructions. It means obeying without delay.

Most importantly, it's important to quickly obey God when He tells you to do something. Psalm 119:60 says, *"I won't waste any time. I will be quick to obey your commands"* (NIRV). Obeying God and others immediately is the only way to obey.

The second way we can honor God with our obedience is to . . .

➡ 2. Obey all the Way!

Have your parents ever told you to clean up your room? Then when you walk in, you realize what a total disaster it is and instead of actually picking up the toys and clothes, you simply shove everything into the closet or under the bed? Is that really obeying what your parents have told you to do? I don't think so.

Obeying means you do what has been asked of you completely. You do exactly what you have been told to do, and you do a good job. Doing something half way isn't obedience.

There's a story in the Bible that shows how God feels about half-way obedience. Moses led the Israelites out of Egypt, and now they were wandering around in the wilderness. It was hot, and they were thirsty! Moses and his brother Aaron prayed and asked God to miraculously provide something for the people to drink. God told Moses to speak to a rock, and then water would flow out of it. (Umm…super cool!)

When Moses got to the rock, he didn't follow God's instructions. He was frustrated with the people and all their grumbling and complaining. Instead of speaking to the rock like God told him to, he hit it with his staff instead. Now, God didn't want to see His people die of thirst, so He caused water to come out of the rock anyway.

But God was not very happy with Moses and Aaron.

Polka Dot Girls ✿ Self-Control

week 8

Numbers 20:12 says, *"God said to Moses and Aaron, 'Because you didn't trust me, didn't treat me with holy reverence in front of the People of Israel, you two aren't going to lead this company into the land that I am giving them.'"* God punished them for not doing exactly what He had told them to do. Not only did they strike the rock instead of speaking to it, they didn't remind the people that the miracle came from God, and they took the glory of the miracle for themselves. Because of their disobedience, they were not able to enter the Promised Land. They were punished because they didn't obey God all the way.

When God asks you to do something, do it until it's complete. When your parents tell you something, follow their instructions. When your teachers or coaches give you directions, do your very best to do what they say. Don't do things halfway—obey all the way.

The last way we can honor God with our obedience is to…

➡ 3. Obey the Right Way.

All of us have been asked to do things that we REALLY don't want to do. We already talked about the idea that God wants us to obey, all the way, without delay. It's also important to obey with a good attitude and good effort.

Sometimes that can be really hard! Maybe your mom told you to clean your room and you obeyed her, but the whole time you were cleaning you stomped your feet and slammed doors. Or maybe you complained and whined the whole time. Or maybe you did the job as slow as possible just because you were trying to make sure everyone knew how UNHAPPY you were that you had to clean your room.

Do you think obeying with a bad attitude is pleasing to God? I don't think so. Of course it's important to follow through even when you don't feel like it, but it's also important to obey with the right heart and actions.

Philippians 2:14 says, "*Do everything without complaining or arguing*" (NIRV). We need to check our attitude while we're obeying. Are we "technically" obeying while throwing a fit? Or, are we working with a good attitude even if it's not our favorite thing to do? God honors a good attitude because it's a sign of respect to those He has put in charge of us.

One last thought about obeying: God wants you to obey your earthly authority, but He wants you to obey His Word first and foremost. If you ever have an authority in your life wanting you to do or say something that goes against God's laws, you need to talk to a trusted adult about the situation. Sometimes adults make mistakes too, and God doesn't want you doing things you know are wrong because you're trying to obey someone who's leading you down the wrong path. Talk to someone you trust, and they'll help you figure out the best way to handle your situation.

Obeying God is more important than anything else in your life. When you listen carefully to the things He tells you to do, doing your very best to do them quickly, thoroughly, and with a good attitude, things will go well for you!

Polka Dot Girls ❀ Self-Control

week 8

Kindergarten and 1st Grade Group Discussion Questions

1. Romans 13:1 says, *"For all authority comes from God, and those in positions of authority have been placed there by God."* Who are some people God has made authorities in your life?

2. Why does God give us these people? What's their job?

3. What does the word OBEY mean?

4. God wants us to obey without delay. Give an example of a time when you didn't obey right away.

5. When we're asked to do something by someone in authority over us, is it okay to only obey part of their instructions? Why is this important?

6. We need to obey with a good attitude. Share a time when you did something you weren't really excited about, but you did it with a good attitude anyway.

Polka Dot Girls ❀ Self-Control

week 8

2nd and 3rd Grade Group Discussion Questions

1. Romans 13:1 says, *"For all authority comes from God, and those in positions of authority have been placed there by God."* Who are some people God has made authorities in your life?

2. Why does God give us these people? What's their job?

3. What does the word OBEY mean?

4. God wants us to obey without delay. Give an example of a time when you didn't obey right away.

5. When we're asked to do something by someone in authority over us, is it okay to only obey part of their instructions? Why is this important?

6. We need to obey with a good attitude. Share a time when you did something you weren't really excited about, but you did it with a good attitude anyway.

Polka Dot Girls ✿ Self-Control

week 8

4th and 5th Grade Group Discussion Questions

1. Romans 13:1 says, *"For all authority comes from God, and those in positions of authority have been placed there by God."* Who are some people God has made authorities in your life?

2. Why does God give us these people? What's their job?

3. What does the word OBEY mean?

4. God wants us to obey without delay. Give an example of a time when you didn't obey right away.

5. When we're asked to do something by someone in authority over us, is it okay to only obey part of their instructions? Why is this important?

6. We need to obey with a good attitude. Share a time when you did something you weren't really excited about, but you did it with a good attitude anyway.

7. Attitude is everything! Why do you think God cares about your attitude? (*Possible Answer: God always cares about our hearts. It's possible to do the right thing the wrong way.*)

Polka Dot Girls ❦ Self-Control

week 8

True Obedience Comes from the Heart!
(EASY VERSION FOR YOUNGER GIRLS)

Supplies Needed:
- White Cardstock (2 sheets per girl)
- Heart Template
- Project Template
- Red and Pink Acrylic Paint
- Pencils with Erasers (1 per girl)

Prep:
- Copy the heart template onto cardstock.
- Cut out the heart template.
- Copy the project template onto cardstock

What Should We Do Next?
- Give each girl a project template and the cut-out heart template.
- Secure the heart template onto the project template with a small piece of tape on the back. (The tape is used to keep the heart template from moving as you paint around it.)
- Dip the pencil eraser into the colored paint.
- Outline the heart template with many dots.
- Go around the heart template as many times as needed.
- Slowly remove the heart template.
- The finished project will be the shape of heart in dots.

With a Happy Heart, God wants us to OBEY, without DELAY, all the way, the RIGHT way!

Polka Dot Girls ❀ Self-Control

week 8

True Obedience Comes from the Heart!
(CHALLENGING VERSION FOR OLDER GIRLS)

<u>Supplies Needed:</u>
- 8x10" Foam Board or Canvas (white or black)
- Silver Flathead Thumbtacks (about 35 per girl)
- Skein of Yarn (or other colored string)
- Hot Glue Gun
- White Cardstock
- Heart Template

<u>Prep:</u>
- Print the heart template onto the white cardstock.
- Cut out the heart.

<u>What Should We Do Next?</u>
- Place the heart template on the foam board or canvas.
- Poke the tacks through dots around the heart.
- When you're finished, carefully peel the heart template off the canvas/foam board, leaving the tacks in place.
- It's okay if a couple of your tacks come out—just pop them back into place. The tacks will be secured later.
- Starting from the bottom, wrap your yarn/string around the bottom tack.
- Weave your way up the heart.
- Wrap the yarn/string around each tack 2–3 times.
- When you get to the top, wrap the yarn/string to one side of the heart and then weave the yarn/string to the other side.
- Cut and tie the yarn/string around one tack.
- If using a canvas, turn the heart over and use your hot glue gun to secure each tack by placing a dab of glue over each tack.

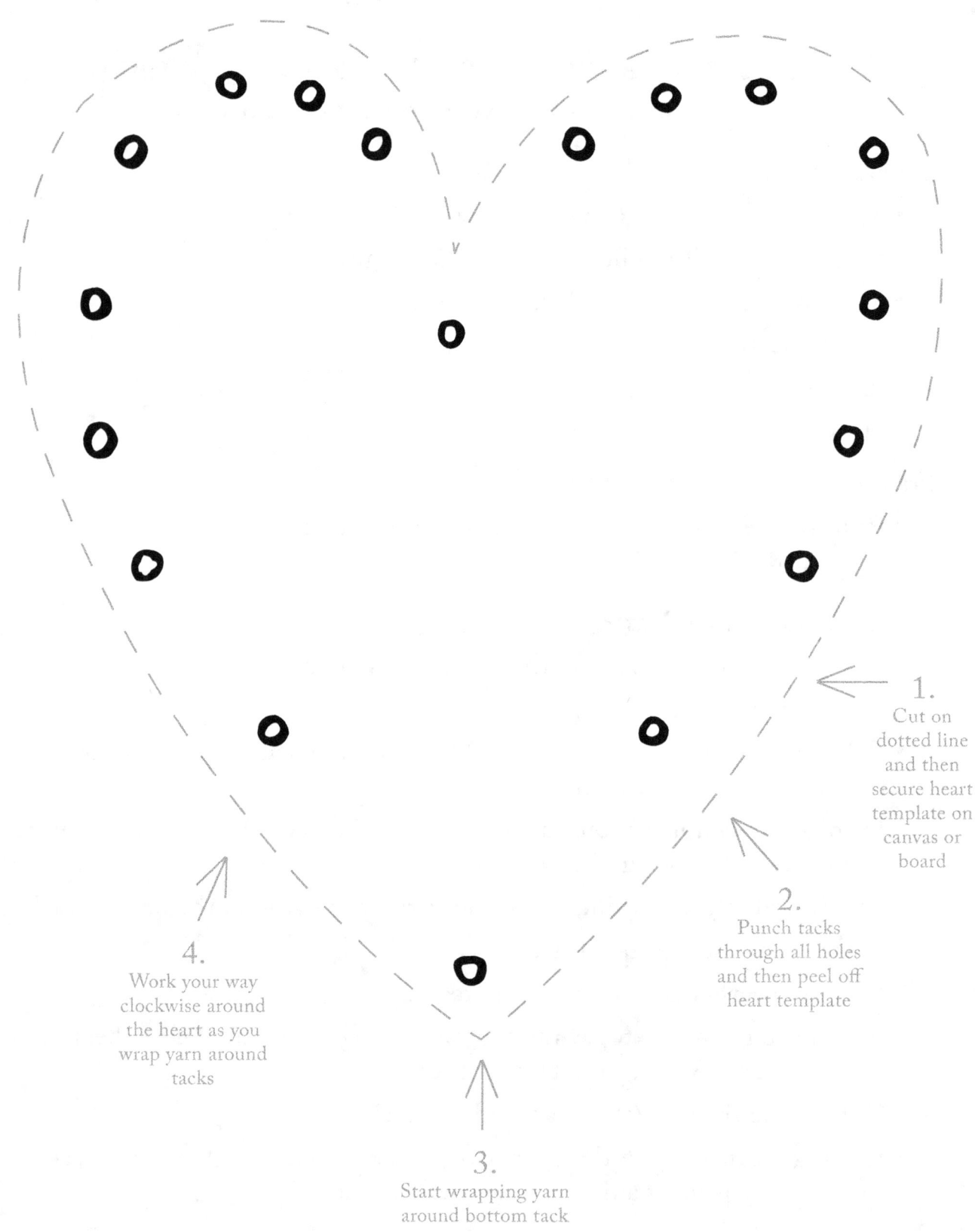

week 8

Parent Partner

Wouldn't it be fantastic if our kids always obeyed us? No procrastinating, no whining, no pretending they've suddenly lost the ability to hear and speak when we ask them to do something. I might actually fall over from shock.

The truth is that obedience doesn't come easily to any of us, especially children. Even if our intentions are to obey, we're often distracted and fail to follow through with what has been asked of us.

This week we talked to the girls about obeying without delay, all the way, the right way. This means that we obey the first time we're asked to do something. We don't wait until it suits us—we obey immediately when someone in authority tells us to do something. Obeying all the way means we do our very best. We complete the task to the best of our abilities. We do it the right way, with a good attitude. No stomping, whining, or complaining allowed!

Our job as parents is to continually prepare our children for the life they will one day encounter outside the walls of our house. One of the most fundamental aspects of a healthy child is their ability to respect and honor what authority has asked them to do. So be patient, be consistent, and keep encouraging them to practice obedience every single day. You won't regret it.

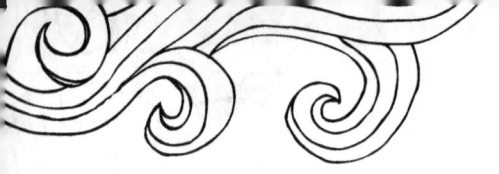

Polka Dot Girls ❦ Self-Control

week 8

Kindergarten and 1st Grade Take Home Activity Sheet

Fill in the blanks with the word OBEY.

Ephesians 6:1 (ERV)

Children, _____ your parents the way the Lord wants, because this is the right thing to do.

Jeremiah 42:6

Whether we like it or not, we will _____ the Lord our God to whom we are sending you with our plea. For if we _____ him, everything will turn out well for us.

Psalm 119:60 (NIRV)

I won't waste any time. I will be quick to _____ your commands.

In the squares write:
Complain, whine, cry, yell, stomp

In the circles write:
Ignore, delay, wait, disobey

In the hearts write:
Obey, without, all, right

Color all the circles green.

Color all the squares blue.

Color all the hearts red.

Now fill in the blanks with the words in the hearts:

God wants us to _____ , _____ delay,

_____ the way, the _____ way!

Polka Dot Girls ❀ Self-Control

week 8

When we obey God, we do what He tells us to. We follow the path He wants us to take instead of choosing our own way. Complete the maze below and remind yourself to choose God's path!

Polka Dot Girls ❀ Self-Control

week 8

2nd and 3rd Grade Take Home Activity Sheets

Fill in the blanks with the word OBEY.

Ephesians 6:1 (ERV)

Children, _____ your parents the way the Lord wants, because this is the right thing to do.

Jeremiah 42:6

Whether we like it or not, we will _____ the Lord our God to whom we are sending you with our plea. For if we _____ him, everything will turn out well for us.

Psalm 119:60 (NIRV)

I won't waste any time. I will be quick to _____ your commands.

In the squares write:
Complain, whine, cry, yell, stomp

In the circles write:
Ignore, delay, wait, disobey

In the hearts write:
Obey, without, all, right

Color all the circles green.

Color all the squares blue.

Color all the hearts red.

Now fill in the blanks with the words in the hearts:

God wants us to _____, _____ delay,

_____ the way, the _____ way!

Polka Dot Girls ❀ Self-Control

week 8

When we obey God, we do what He tells us to. We follow the path He wants us to take instead of choosing our own way. Complete the maze below and remind yourself to choose God's path!

START

FINISH!

Polka Dot Girls ❖ Self-Control

week 8

4th and 5th Grade Take Home Activity Sheets

Look up the following verses in your Bible and underline them with a pretty color pencil. Then write them out in the space provided. Write out one way you can follow the truth in your own life in the heart next to each verse.

Ephesians 6:1

Jeremiah 42:6

Psalm 119:60

Do you remember what we learned today? Fill in the blanks.

God wants us to _____, _____ delay, _____ the way, the _____ way!

When we obey God, we do what He tells us to. We follow the path He wants us to take instead of choosing our own way. Complete the maze below and remind yourself to choose God's path!

START ↓

↑ FINISH!

Polka Dot Girls ❀ Self-Control

Self-Control
week 9

Your Body, God's House

WHAT'S THE POINT?
OUR BODIES ARE GOD'S HOUSE, AND WE NEED TO TAKE GOOD CARE OF HIS HOUSE!

theme verse
You know that you are God's house. The spirit of God lives in you.
1 Corinthians 3:16 (WE)

related bible passage
Daniel 1:8–19

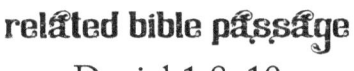

❋ Large Group Lesson ❋

What does your house look like? Do you have your own room, or do you share with someone? Did you get to decorate your room a certain way? The place where we live is a very special—it's where we spend time with our family, where we come to rest and relax, where we get away from all the craziness of the world. It's the special place that belongs to us and the people we love.

I don't know about you, but there's nothing I love more than coming home after a long, busy day and walking into my house, where I can smell yummy things cooking and see all the things and people I love. Our homes are important!

Did you know God has a house? It's true—He does! It might surprise you to learn where God's house is. It's not a church or a big mansion. It's actually YOU! The Bible tells us the spirit of God lives inside of us in 1 Corinthians 3:16: *"You know that you are God's house. The spirit of God lives in you"* (WE). When we ask Jesus to come into our life, He makes His home inside of us. He lives in us and helps us in every way possible. What a cool thought!

Since God's house is inside our bodies, don't you think it's important for us to take care of our bodies? What would happen to your real house if you never took care of it, if you never took out the trash or cleaned up the dishes? What if you never painted the outside or made sure the grass was mowed? It wouldn't take long before your house would be broken down, messed up, and not very much fun to live in.

Just like we take care of our physical houses, we need to take care of our bodies—God's house!

What are some ways you can take good care of God's house?

⇨ 1. Take Good Care of your Body.

Samantha was so excited to FINALLY be on summer vacation—no more getting up early to catch the bus, no more homework, no more school lunches! She couldn't wait to just lie around and relax.

She started staying up WAY too late every night. She would sneak a flashlight into her room and read her book well into the night. Then she'd sleep in late and stumble down into the kitchen and pour herself a bowl of super-sugary cereal and eat a couple doughnuts. Then she laid on the couch, watching TV for the rest of the morning. She forgot to brush her teeth and decided she'd get to it later. She even forgot to take a shower like her mom told her to do.

By the time dinner rolled around, Samantha wasn't feeling so great. Her body was NOT happy with her. Her muscles ached, her tummy hurt, and she felt pretty blah. She realized that, although it sounds fun to be lazy and eat junk all day long, it really made her feel horrible! She decided to go to bed early and try to do better the next day.

Polka Dot Girls ❀ Self-Control

God wants you to take good care of your body! That means eating healthy foods, getting plenty of exercise, brushing your teeth every day, and taking baths or showers to make sure that your body stays clean. Taking care of God's house means taking good care of your body!

The second way you can take good care of your bodies is to . . .

➡ 2. Put Good Things into your Body!

Have you ever watched your mom or dad put gas in the car? The gas is the fuel that makes the car work! Your body works the same way—what you put inside it determines how well your body works. Your food is supposed to give your body power.

There are two kinds of food we can put into our bodies: lazy foods and power foods. Lazy foods are full of sugar and fat. They might taste good, but they don't give us any power. Lazy foods include sugary cereals, candy, fast food, and other greasy things.

Power foods fill our bodies with good things that build up our muscles and give us energy. They're filled with vitamins and minerals and protein that give our bodies the fuel they need to work hard. Power foods make your body healthy and strong! Some yummy power foods are fruits, vegetables, nuts, whole grains and lean meat.

When you're choosing the foods you put in your body, choose power foods over lazy foods. Your body will thank you!

The last way you can take good care of your bodies is to...

➡ 3. Practice Self-Control When you Make your Food Choices.

I know it seems like a really good idea to eat ten cookies for breakfast, but is that really a good choice? Sometimes we open a bag of candy and just can't seem to help ourselves from eating every last piece right before dinner. It's just so yummy!

One of the biggest areas where we need to practice self-control throughout our lives is what we eat. Your tummy might be screaming loudly, "EAT MORE SUGAR! GIVE ME MORE DONUTS! DON'T EAT THOSE VEGETABLES! GIVE ME POTATO CHIPS INSTEAD!" In that moment, you have to use your self-control to make a better choice to eat things that make your body healthy.

Here's a fun way to help yourself practice self-control with your food—try using the "Go-Slow-Whoa" trick when choosing your food.

GO foods are the very best POWER foods—foods that are always a good idea: fruits, veggies, water, and healthy protein like lean meats, yogurt, and nuts. Choose GO foods for most of your daily meals and snacks. Your body will be full of power and energy when you give it this kind of food.

SLOW foods are foods that are good to eat sometimes. They're not really bad for you, but you should only eat them occasionally. They're higher in fat and sugar and have more calories. SLOW foods include breads and pastas, cheese, and processed foods. Slow foods still have some nutrition in them, but your diet shouldn't only include SLOW foods.

And then there are WHOA foods. These are for special occasions. They're high in sugar and fat and don't have much nutritional value. It's okay to have cake or ice cream every once in a while, but if you eat too much too often, your body won't have any energy. If your diet is full of WHOA foods, your body won't be working as well as it should be.

Polka Dot Girls ❀ Self-Control

week 9

ILLUSTRATION: GO! SLOW! WHOA! Relay

Set out a variety of food items on two tables, making sure there's the same number of items on each table. Include GO foods, WHOA foods, and SLOW Foods. Place three baskets or buckets in front of each table. Label them with GO, SLOW, and WHOA.

Divide the girls into two teams and line them up on the opposite end of the room. When the game starts, the girls should take turns running to the food table, selecting an item, and dropping it in the appropriate basket. The first team to empty their table wins.

Remember, your body is God's house. He made our bodies, and He wants us to take good care of them! Psalm 100:3 says, "*Know that the Lord is God. He made us, and we belong to Him.*" When we remember that our bodies belong to God, we'll want to make sure they're as strong and healthy as they can be. This is a great way to show God you're glad He lives inside of you.

Polka Dot Girls ❦ Self-Control

week 9

Kindergarten and 1st Grade Group Discussion Questions

1. The places we live are very important to us. What's one way you help take care of your home?

2. What does the Bible say about where God lives? (*Answer: Our bodies are God's house!*)

3. Let's practice saying our theme verse together!
   You know that you are God's house. The spirit of God lives in you.
   —1 Corinthians 3:16 (WE)

4. What are some ways you can take good care of your body?

5. Why is it important to eat power foods instead of lazy foods?

6. What are the three kinds of foods we talked about today? Which one do you like to eat the most? What can you do this week to make better food choices?

Polka Dot Girls ♣ Self-Control

week 9

2nd and 3rd Grade Group Discussion Questions

1. The places we live are very important to us. What's one way you help take care of your home?

2. What does the Bible say about where God lives? (*Answer: Our bodies are God's house!*)

3. Let's practice saying our theme verse together!
   You know that you are God's house. The spirit of God lives in you.
   —1 Corinthians 3:16 (WE)

4. What are some ways you can take good care of your body?

5. Why is it important to eat power foods instead of lazy foods?

6. What are the three kinds of foods we talked about today? Which one do you like to eat the most? What can you do this week to make better food choices?

7. Sometimes we can feel embarrassed about our bodies or think they should look different than they do, but God made all of our bodies different! Does being healthy mean everyone's body needs to look the same?

Polka Dot Girls ❦ Self-Control

week 9

4th and 5th Grade Group Discussion Questions

1. The places we live are very important to us. What's one way you help take care of your home?

2. What does the Bible say about where God lives? (*Answer: Our bodies are God's house!*)

3. Let's practice saying our theme verse together!
   You know that you are God's house. The spirit of God lives in you.
   —1 Corinthians 3:16 (WE)

4. What are some ways you can take good care of your body?

5. Sometimes we can feel embarrassed about our bodies or think they should look different than they do, but God made all of our bodies different! Does being healthy mean everyone's body needs to look the same?

6. Taking good care of our bodies means accepting and loving the way God made us. What's one thing that you like about the way you look?

7. Why is it important to eat power foods instead of lazy foods?

8. Using self-control when it comes to your food is very important. Have you ever stopped yourself from eating too much of one thing or chosen a heathy snack instead of a sugary snack? What was that like?

9. What are the three kinds of foods we talked about today? Which one do you like to eat the most? What can you do this week to make better food choices?

Polka Dot Girls ❖ Self-Control

week 9

Strengthen Your Faith Workout!

<u>Supplies Needed:</u>
- Paper Cups (2 per girl)
- Permanent Marker
- Popsicle Sticks (12–15 per girl)
- Stickers (optional)

<u>What Should We Do Next?</u>
- Give each girl 2 paper cups.
- Tell the girls to write "Daily Workout" on one cup and "Done!" on the other cup.
- Decorate the cups with pretty stickers.
- Give each girl 12–15 popsicle sticks.
- On each popsicle stick, instruct the girls to write different exercises. For example:
  - Push-ups (10)
  - Jumping Jacks (25)
  - Running in Place (2 minutes)
  - Squats (25)
  - Burpees (15)

Instructions: Exercise your body and your faith each day! Each day, pull out several popsicle sticks and do the exercises listed on them. When you're finished with an exercise, place it in the "Done!" cup.

Parent Partner

Oh man. This one's gonna be tough. When it comes to teaching our kids self-control in the way they take care of their bodies, we can't just say, "Do as I say, not as I do." If I'm honest, this is one of the greatest areas of struggle in my life, and it can be something I easily brush off and ignore in my parenting.

We want our kids to learn healthy habits and make good decisions NOW. We need them to understand the importance of taking good care of their bodies while they're young—it certainly doesn't get easier as they get older!

Today we taught the girls that our bodies are the house God lives in, and we need to take good care of His house! We do this by brushing our teeth, keeping our bodies clean, getting enough rest, etc.

We also taught the girls the difference between foods that give our bodies energy—power foods—and foods that fill our bodies but don't offer anything nutritious—lazy foods. The girls should fill their bodies with power foods that will help them grow big and strong!

We also taught the girls the GO-SLOW-WHOA principle. GO foods include fruits, vegetables, lean proteins, and dairy. Their diets should consist mostly of these healthy foods. SLOW foods include carbs, healthy fats, and other foods that are fine in moderation. WHOA foods are the things we should eat sparingly or on special occasions, like ice cream or french fries. I love this concept because it doesn't rule out foods, but it helps the girls recognize what should make up the bulk of their diet.

We all want our kids to be healthy! Teaching them to take care of their bodies is a lifelong skill that they will thank you for later.

week 9

Kindergarten and 1st Grade Take Home Activity Sheets

The Bible says our bodies are God's house. Each one of us has a body that is unique and beautiful, just the way God made us. Color and decorate this house with your favorite colors and shapes. Make it special, just like you!

We show God we love Him by taking care of the bodies He has given us. Circle the pictures of things that are healthy for our bodies.

Polka Dot Girls ❀ Self-Control

week 9

2nd and 3rd Grade Take Home Activity Sheets

The Bible says our bodies are God's house. Each one of us has a body that is unique and beautiful, just the way God made us. Color and decorate this house with your favorite colors and shapes. Make it special, just like you!

Use the key to solve the word problem below.

1 Corinthians 3:16 (WE)

A	B	C	D	E	F	G	H	I	J	K	L	M	N	O	P	R	S	T	U	V	W	Y
19	9	12	5	21	20	1	17	25	4	3	2	13	16	18	8	10	11	7	14	6	26	22

__ __ __   __ __ __ __   __ __ __ __   __ __ __
22 18 14   3 16 18 26   7 17 19 7   22 18 14

__ __ __   __ __ __ '   __   __ __ __ __ __ .
19 10 21   1 18 5   11   17 18 14 11 21

__ __ __   __ __ __ __ __ __   __ __ __
7 17 21   11 8 25 10 25 7   18 20   1 18 5

__ __ __ __ __   __ __   __ __ __ .
2 25 6 21 11   25 16   22 18 14

We can make healthy choices when it comes to the food we put into our bodies. In the space below, list some things that are **GO** foods, **SLOW** foods, and **WHOA** foods.

GO	SLOW	WHOA

Polka Dot Girls ❀ Self-Control

week 9

4th and 5th Grade Take Home Activity Sheets

Solve the puzzle below to remind yourself where God lives.

1 Corinthians 3:16 (WE)

A	B	C	D	E	F	G	H	I	J	K	L	M	N	O	P	R	S	T	U	V	W	Y
19	9	12	5	21	20	1	17	25	4	3	2	13	16	18	8	10	11	7	14	6	26	22

__ __ __   __ __ __ __   __ __ __ __   __ __ __
22 18 14   3 16 18 26   7 17 19 7   22 18 14

__ __ __   __ __ __ '   __ __   __ __ __ __ __ __.
19 10 21   1 18 5   11   17 18 14 11 21

__ __ __   __ __ __ __ __ __ __   __ __ __   __ __ __
7 17 21   11 8 25 10 25 7   18 20   1 18 5

__ __ __ __ __   __ __ __   __ __ __.
2 25 6 21 11   25 16   22 18 14

We can make healthy choices when it comes to the food we put into our bodies. In the space below, list some things that are **GO** foods, **SLOW** foods, and **WHOA** foods.

GO	SLOW	WHOA

As we get older, we can sometimes feel bad about how our bodies feel different. It's important to remind yourself that God created your body unique and different on purpose. He wants your body to be healthy, but that doesn't mean every body will look the same. Look up Psalm 139:14 and write it out in the space provided. Then make a list of the ways God made your body unique (things like hair color, eye color, skin color, and any other thing that makes you YOU).

Psalm 139:14

Uniquely Me!

Polka Dot Girls ❖ Self-Control

Self-Control
week 10

Hands and Feet

WHAT'S THE POINT?
OUR BODIES BELONG TO GOD AND WE NEED TO USE THEM THE WAY HE WANTS US TO!

theme verse

But I discipline my body and keep it under control.
1 Corinthians 9:27

related bible passage

Romans 6:12–14

❖ Large Group Lesson ❖

Last week we talked about the fact that our bodies are God's house. The Bible says He lives inside of us, so we need to take good care of His house. We should be taking good care of our bodies by exercising, eating good foods, and making sure we stay clean and healthy.

Today we're going to talk more about practicing self-control with our bodies. We need to make sure every part of us is behaving in a way that shows others we belong to God.

Can you think of a time when it seemed like your body was in control of you? Maybe you could NOT stay awake during class or church. No matter how hard you tried, your eyes would NOT stay open. Your body wanted to sleep, and it seemed like nothing you did kept you awake!

Or maybe you were REALLY hungry and your stomach kept growling and growling. No matter how hard you tried NOT to, all you could think about was a double cheeseburger with extra bacon and cheese, and your stomach got louder and louder until everyone could hear it.

Or maybe you had to go to the bathroom really, really bad and you just kept jumping and dancing around thinking, "I can wait! I'm having so much fun with my friends. I don't want to stop playing to go inside." Pretty soon you realize that you better go NOW because your body is going to take over and you're going to go to the bathroom whether or not you're IN the bathroom.

Our bodies can sure be bossy. Sometimes we find ourselves in a situation where we do something with our bodies that we know isn't right. If we wanted to, we could stop ourselves, but we just don't practice self-control.

Have you ever done something with your hands that hurt another person? Maybe you hit your little sister or took something from your neighbor that didn't belong to you. Maybe you wrote something mean about another person or pushed someone because they made you mad.

Have you ever let your feet take you into a situation that you knew wasn't good? Maybe you went over to a friend's house even though you knew your mom had told you not to. Maybe you ran away from a friend who wanted to play with you and hurt her feelings by excluding her. Maybe you stomped your feet in a temper tantrum because you didn't get your way. Or maybe you kicked the door to your bedroom when your mom grounded you for having a bad attitude.

Proverbs 6:18 tells us that God HATES *"feet that are quick to do wrong."* Does that mean that God doesn't like feet? Of course not! It means God doesn't like it when we let our feet take us places that will get us into trouble.

Polka Dot Girls ❀ Self-Control

week 10

We need to keep our bodies under control. God wants our hands and feet to do good things for Him, not things that could hurt other people or disobey our parents.

What are some things you can do to practice self-control with your body?

You need to...

➡ 1. Think Before you act.

Sometimes we do things with our bodies before we stop to think about our actions. Have you ever heard the word "impulsive"? It means you do something before you stop and think.

Instead of reacting in the moment when you're mad or sad or angry, try stopping yourself BEFORE you act. Take a deep breath and count to three. Then think about your actions and possible consequences. Are you going to hurt someone? Are you going to make someone sad? Think about how YOU would feel if the same thing was done to you, THEN make a good choice regarding your actions.

Another smart idea is to ask yourself a few questions before you act. What will happen if you do the thing you're thinking about doing? What will happen if you DON'T do the thing you're thinking about doing? Look at both choices and decide which is the better option.

Ephesians 5:17 says, "*Don't act thoughtlessly, but understand what the Lord wants you to do.*" When you act before you think, you're acting thoughtlessly. Stop yourself before you act and ask God if this action will be pleasing to Him. Then make the choice to honor God with your actions.

I know it can be REALLY hard to stop yourself when you want to react to something, but it can take just SECONDS to say or do something that will have lasting effects on you and others. Don't let your actions happen before you have a chance to think about them. Stop and think. Then act.

The second way we can have self-control with our bodies is to . . .

➡ 2. Respect Other People's Bodies

God gave each one of us a body, and He cares about us! He wants us to care about other people, too. When you do something that hurts or bothers another person, that isn't pleasing to God.

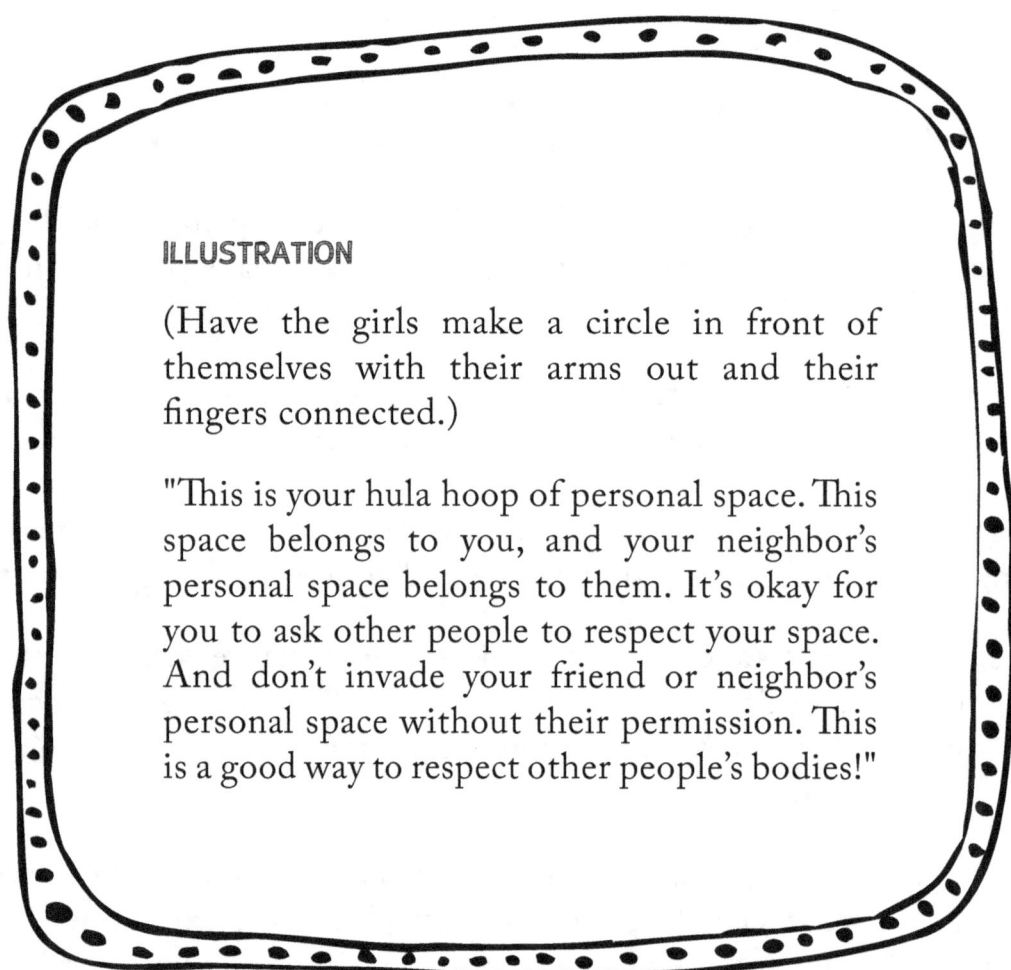

ILLUSTRATION

(Have the girls make a circle in front of themselves with their arms out and their fingers connected.)

"This is your hula hoop of personal space. This space belongs to you, and your neighbor's personal space belongs to them. It's okay for you to ask other people to respect your space. And don't invade your friend or neighbor's personal space without their permission. This is a good way to respect other people's bodies!"

There was a boy in Abby's class who always bothered her. He pulled her pony tails in class and pinched her arm at recess. Sometimes he would try to distract her by making funny noises during quizzes. One day he pushed her down on the playground and she finally had enough.

"You better stop this right now!" she said loudly to the boy. "You are always in my personal space, and if you don't stop it right now, I'm going to talk to the teacher and make sure you get into trouble." The boy walked away laughing, but Abby felt good that she had stood up for herself.

week 10

Your body belongs to you. No one else should bother you, hurt you, or do things that make you feel uncomfortable. In the same way, you should always respect other people's bodies. Be kind and careful when you're playing games. Don't push or shove others. Don't distract others by poking them, throwing things, or doing anything else that could keep them from doing their best when they're trying to concentrate.

Philippians 2:3 says, "*In whatever you do, don't let selfishness or pride be your guide. Be humble, and honor others more than yourselves*" (ERV). God wants you to care about other people, and that includes respecting their bodies.

The last way you can practice self-control with your body is to…

⇒ 3. Keep your Body under Control.

> ILLUSTRATION: Bubble Popping Exercise
>
> You can either have a few volunteers come forward for this exercise, or if your group is small, do it with the whole group.
>
> Take a bottle of bubbles and tell the kids you're going to blow bubbles at them. Their job is to remain perfectly still and not catch, stomp, pop, or doing anything else to the bubbles.
>
> This is a great example of what it means to practice self-control with their bodies!

That was hard, wasn't it? It's not easy to keep your body under control, but that is exactly what you need to do every single day. First Corinthians 9:27 says, *"But I discipline my body and keep it under control."* God wants us to be in charge of what our bodies do. This means practicing self-control instead of letting our bodies do whatever comes to mind.

You can practice self-control with your body when you choose NOT to hit someone when you get angry with them. You can practice self-control when you refuse to throw a tantrum even though you're disappointed that your parents won't let you do something. You can practice self-control when you respond to your sister with a calm, quiet voice instead of yelling at her. You can practice self-control with your body by sitting still when the teacher has asked you not to get up from your desk. None of these things are easy, but you can do them! God has promised to help you practice self-control. If you pray and ask God for His help, He has promised to give you the strength to be disciplined with your actions.

week 10

Kindergarten and 1st Grade Group Discussion Questions

1. Sometimes our bodies are bossy! Name a time when your body was trying really hard to be in control.

2. If we're not careful, our bodies can hurt other people. Name some ways we can hurt others with our hands. Name some ways we can hurt others with our feet.

3. What are some ways we can think before we act? (*Possible Answers: Count to three, take deep breaths before we say or do something, think about what will happen if you do/don't do this thing.*)

4. What are some ways you can respect other people's bodies by controlling your own body? (*Possible Answers: Hula hoop of personal space, think about how your actions will make others feel.*)

5. Name one way you're going to keep your body under control this week.

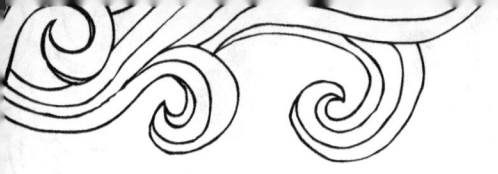

Polka Dot Girls ❀ Self-Control

week 10

2nd and 3rd Grade Group Discussion Questions

1. Sometimes our bodies are bossy! Name a time when your body was trying really hard to be in control.

2. If we're not careful, our bodies can hurt other people. Name some ways we can hurt others with our hands. Name some ways we can hurt others with our feet.

3. What are some ways we can think before we act? (*Possible Answers: Count to three, take deep breaths before we say or do something, think about what will happen if you do/don't do this thing.*)

4. What are some ways you can respect other people's bodies by controlling your own body? (*Possible Answers: Hula hoop of personal space, think about how your actions will make others feel.*)

5. Why do you think the Bible says God "hates feet that are quick to do wrong"? How should this affect the things we choose to do with our friends?

6. Name one way you're going to keep your body under control this week.

Polka Dot Girls ❀ Self-Control

week 10

4th and 5th Grade Group Discussion Questions

1. Sometimes our bodies are bossy! Name a time when your body was trying really hard to be in control.

2. If we're not careful, our bodies can hurt other people. Name some ways we can hurt others with our hands. Name some ways we can hurt others with our feet.

3. Take a minute to think about the things we could WRITE about others with our hands. Maybe it's a note for a friend or something you write online about someone else. How should we approach the things we write? How can we make sure we're not harming people with our hands?

4. What are some ways we can think before we act? (*Possible Answers: Count to three, take deep breaths before we say or do something, think about what will happen if you do/don't do this thing.*)

5. What are some ways you can respect other people's bodies by controlling your own body? (*Possible Answers: Hula hoop of personal space, think about how your actions will make others feel.*)

6. Why do you think the Bible says God "hates feet that are quick to do wrong"? How should this affect the things we choose to do with our friends?

7. Name one way you're going to keep your body under control this week.

Polka Dot Girls ✿ Self-Control

week 10

Serve One Another in LOVE!

<u>Supplies Needed:</u>
- Large Canvas or Tag Board
- Tempura Paint in a Variety of Colors
- Paint Brushes
- Newspaper or Cheap Table Cloth
- Paper Towel for Clean-up
- Embellishments (optional)

<u>What Should We Do?</u>
- Paint the letter "L" on the left side of the canvas or tag board.
- Have each girl paint her hand and use a handprint to create the "O" in love.
- Paint the girls' feet and use footprints to create the "V" in love.
- Finish the word by painting the letter "E".
- Decorate the canvas or tag board with pretty embellishments.
- For larger groups, it may be easier to paint the letter "V" rather than using footprints.

Parent Partner

I'm sure I'm not the only parent who has said, "Keep your hands to yourself!" a million times. Kids are busy and impulsive, and if they're not careful, their hands and feet can get them into trouble!

We're all impulsive to some extent, but one of the greatest lessons we must learn as we're growing up is to control our compulsions and discipline our actions. This week we talked to the girls about controlling their hands and feet. This involves the actions of their hands and feet, as well as being careful about where their feet are taking them.

We reminded them that they should stop and think before they act. They may need to take a few deep breaths or count to three before they respond. We encouraged them to think through the consequences of their actions BEFORE they act. If they can give themselves a minute to calm down and process the ramifications of their behavior, the chances of them making a good choice go up significantly.

Then we talked about respecting other people's bodies. This includes not hitting, kicking, or distracting others as well as honoring their personal space.

We also taught the girls to practice controlling their bodies instead of simply reacting and doing whatever comes to them compulsively. Intentionally keeping our bodies under control is something we all need to do.

It may take some time, but if your daughter will put in the practice, she can become disciplined with her hands and feet!

week 10

Kindergarten and 1st Grade Take Home Activity Pages

Write the word **BODY** in the blank spaces below.

But don't let sin control your life here on earth. You must not be ruled by the things your sinful self makes you want to do. Don't offer the parts of your _____ to serve sin. Don't use your _____ to do evil, but offer yourselves to God, as people who have died and now live. Offer the parts of your _____ to God to be used for doing good. – Romans 6:12–13 (ERV)

Today we learned that we should think before we act. In the scenarios below, circle the **RIGHT** way to act in each situation.

1. Someone takes your toy:

    a. Hitting back   b. Asking for toy back

2. Your sister is being annoying:

    a. Kick your sister   b. Walk away

3. You don't get the candy you want at the store:

    a. Throw a tantrum   b. Be sad but accept it

4. You lose at softball:

    a. Cry "It's not fair, you cheated!"   b. Shake hands with other team and say "Good job"

We need to respect other people's bodies and personal space. Philippians 2:3 says, "*In whatever you do, don't let selfishness or pride be your guide. Be humble, and honor others more than yourselves*" (ERV).

Find the hidden words below.

R	I	H	X	E	A	R	E
V	P	O	C	N	T	M	L
D	G	M	X	E	M	O	B
S	D	H	D	Y	K	P	M
G	Z	I	M	A	L	O	U
X	R	H	O	N	O	R	H
P	S	V	H	F	H	P	L
H	P	M	X	E	S	D	G

Word List:

Humble

Honor

Pride

Polka Dot Girls ❋ Self-Control

week 10

2nd and 3rd Grade Take Home Activity Pages

Some key words are missing in the verse beliw. Using the first letter of the word as a clue, fill in the missing words using the key below.

But don't let sin C_____ your life here on earth. You must not be ruled by the things your S_____ self makes you want to do. Don't offer the parts of your B_____ to serve sin. Don't use your B_____ to do evil, but offer Y_____ to God, as people who have died and now live. Offer the parts of your B_____ to God to be used for doing G_____.

– Romans 6:12–13 (ERV)

Word List

Good	*Yourselves*	*Sinful*
Body	*Control*	

Today we learned that we should think before we act. In the scenarios below, circle the **RIGHT** way to act in each situation.

1. Someone takes your toy:
   a. Hitting back b. Asking for toy back

2. Your sister is being annoying:
   a. Kick your sister b. Walk away

3. You don't get the candy you want at the store:
   a. Throw a tantrum b. Be sad but accept it

4. You lose at softball:
   a. Cry "It's not fair, you cheated!" b. Shake hands with other team and say "Good job"

We need to respect other people's bodies and personal space. Philippians 2:3 says, "*In whatever you do, don't let selfishness or pride be your guide. Be humble, and honor others more than yourselves*" (ERV).

Find the hidden words below.

```
I O V H R Q E P M W D C D Q O
P Q I O Z O K T M T U K D G C
L E D I R P N N W B J R W B U
K C M I F G H O C P I U Z K A
R M N X N H V Z H H G D Z X X
Y L H A U E P X Z Q U C G H T
S E L M P C V E U F U Q P O R
U U B Q S A F G R H O O P I E
H L S E P P P A C S R J Y U S
E H N Z P S F X M J O M X J P
A Q B H N R T Y O V Q N P D E
V T Z V J L J T T Z U L A Y C
X U S E L F I S H N E S S L T
E R I E M X O Z W P B Y X R L
D M C D N F K T H K M A W V J
```

Word List:

Honor	*Hoop*	*Hula*
Humble	*Personal*	*Pride*
Respect	*Selfishness*	*Space*

Polka Dot Girls ❀ Self-Control

week 10

4th and 5th Grade
Take Home Activity Pages

Look up Romans 6:12–13 in your Bible and write it in the space provided.

Today we learned we need to think before we act. For each scenario below, write out the wrong way to react and the right way to act.

1. Someone steals your spot in line.

2. Your sister is driving you crazy and you just want her to leave you alone.

3. Your friend didn't invite you to her party and your feelings are hurt.

4. You lose the championship game and you're really upset.

5. Your brother takes the last Fruit Roll-Up and he KNEW you wanted it.

Polka Dot Girls ✿ Self-Control

week 10

We need to respect other people's bodies and personal space. Philippians 2:3 says, "*In whatever you do, don't let selfishness or pride be your guide. Be humble, and honor others more than yourselves*" (ERV).

Find the hidden words below.

```
I  O  V  H  R  Q  E  P  M  W  D  C  D  Q  O
P  Q  I  O  Z  O  K  T  M  T  U  K  D  G  C
L  E  D  I  R  P  N  N  W  B  J  R  W  B  U
K  C  M  I  F  G  H  O  C  P  I  U  Z  K  A
R  M  N  X  N  H  V  Z  H  H  G  D  Z  X  X
Y  L  H  A  U  E  P  X  Z  Q  U  C  G  H  T
S  E  L  M  P  C  V  E  U  F  U  Q  P  O  R
U  U  B  Q  S  A  F  G  R  H  O  O  P  I  E
H  L  S  E  P  P  P  A  C  S  R  J  Y  U  S
E  H  N  Z  P  S  F  X  M  J  O  M  X  J  P
A  Q  B  H  N  R  T  Y  O  V  Q  N  P  D  E
V  T  Z  V  J  L  J  T  T  Z  U  L  A  Y  C
X  U  S  E  L  F  I  S  H  N  E  S  S  L  T
E  R  I  E  M  X  O  Z  W  P  B  Y  X  R  L
D  M  C  D  N  F  K  T  H  K  M  A  W  V  J
```

Word List:

Honor   *Hoop*   *Hula*

Humble   *Personal*   *Pride*

Respect   *Selfishness*   *Space*

251

www.ingramcontent.com/pod-product-compliance
Lightning Source LLC
Chambersburg PA
CBHW080847020526
44118CB00037B/2275